HEALING

GOD'S UNCHANGING WILL

A BIBLICAL STUDY FOR THE BASIS OF
PHYSICAL HEALING AS PART OF GOD'S WILL

CARLOS EDUARDO DA COSTA

Healing - God's Unchanging Will
A biblical study for the basis of physical healing as part of God's will
Second Edition
Copyright © 2017 by Carlos Eduardo da Costa
ISBN: 978-0-9993674-0-7

All scriptures quotations, unless otherwise indicated, are taken from the American King James Version. Produced by Michael Peter (Stone) Engelbrite. In public domain since November 8, 1999.

Strong's Greek references are taken from BibleHub.com

For comments, questions, testimonies and requests:

www.CarlosEduardoDaCosta.com
www.facebook.com/healing.godswill
healing@carloseduardodacosta.com

Dedication

I dedicate this book to my awesome parents Fernando Corner da Costa and Carmen Eleonora Pereira da Costa, and my fiancé Aline da Costa Nascimento.

I would like to thank my Christians friends and family that prayed for me before I came to know Jesus: Gabriel Cordeiro, André Lordello, Ricardo Botticelli, my father Fernando da Costa and my stepmother Lury Nagato.

Thank all those who through their writings, teachings and videos are contributing for my growth in the Word: Andrew Wommack, Bill Johnson, Pete Cabrera Jr., Dan Mohler, Todd White, Robby Dawkins, Thomas Fisher, Ravi Zacharias, Francis Chan, the *School of Power and Love* and my pastor, Gary Taylor.

Special thanks to Pauline Clarke-Richards, Jean Morris, Angela Plummer Jones, Christina Belloff and Tamela Holmes who generously contributed by proofreading and correcting the English in this book.

Contents

Preface

This book started with the idea of becoming nothing more than my personal study of the Word of God, I never intended nor imagined I would ever write a book, because when I look to my natural abilities, writing (*and reading*) was never my *forte*, at all. But God will call us to do things that we may think we are not suitable for, things that make us go out of our comfort zones, so that we stop relying on our *own gifts* and start relying on Him, in His Spirit.

Since God put in my heart to expand the 18-page study I did about healing, I've been spending a long time meditating in His Word, developing it, and it amazes me to see what God can do through any person who has a heart for Him and is obedient to His calling. It is not about our own ability but our availability.

We, as Christians, **cannot** live only out of other people's experiences with God. Yes, we can profit from them, but ultimately we need to be meditating on His Word until it becomes our own personal revelation, otherwise we will always be 'baby' Christians who depend on other people's faith to intercede for us, pray for us and heal us — never eating solid food but only drinking milk. I am not saying that it is wrong to go to another believer and ask for prayer, if someone is *weak* or is having difficulties believing for something I would definitely encourage them to ask for help, to get someone to agree in the matter according to scripture; someone to come alongside to build up his or her faith and help them receive what God already provided by grace. My concern is that many Christians do **not** want to pursue a deep relationship with God. They rely on other Christians' *gifts* to 'mediate' between them and God; rather than seek God directly by the way of the same Holy Spirit who abides inside of them.

Healing was always something God put in my heart, since I decided to follow Christ after my own experience with healing. So I would like to briefly share my testimony of how through the manifestation of the goodness and grace of God, I surrendered my life to Him.

I was not raised in a Christian family, I believed in a religion called "Kardecism", also known as a form of Spiritism, very popular in Brazil, which believes in things like karma and reincarnation. Followers of this religion usually call themselves *'Christians'* because they use parts of the teachings of Christ, having even their own book called *"The Gospel according to Spiritism"* in which spirits through channeling interpreted parts of the New Testament. Kardecists teach and practice a lot of charity, and good deeds, they acknowledge Christ as a *great teacher* and as *the most evolved spirit* manifested on Earth, but deny the deity of Christ and his redemptive work on the cross, as the one who paid the price, as our Lord and Savior, so our sins could be forgiven.

Although I had friends who were Christians, it was not until the age of 30, in 2007, that I met the **real** Jesus. In this year not only was I having some stomach issues, *gastritis*, but had *tendinitis* in both hands due to the excessive use of the computer. Since I worked in the computer most part of the day and also played piano as a profession, you can imagine that *tendinitis* had a great impact on me. So I did what most people would do, I went to the doctors: medicine helped a little the stomach and physiotherapy had effect during the sessions, giving some relief in my hands, but since I could not stop working, the relief was temporary.

At this point I accepted the invitation of my Christian friend Gabriel Cordeiro and went to the prayer meeting he had in his house. It was like a family reunion, frequented by people like me that would never go to a conventional evangelical church, especially because of the stigma evangelicals have in Brazil. The meeting started with a praise time, singing songs, then a teaching of the Bible and a final prayer. At this prayer time there were two ladies, Mercedes and Grace, who would go around praying and prophesying over each person. Well, at that time I didn't know anything about prophetic gifts [*gracings*], words of wisdom and words knowledge, as described in the Bible, but I could see the impact it had in those who were there. Those two humble ladies would speak and many would begin to cry, since it was precisely the problems they were going through, they would also speak words to comfort and strengthen; not only that, they would prophesy things to come in people's lives.

On this first day, Mercedes turned to me and said: "*God is showing me a problem in your stomach, kidneys and liver. But there is no need to worry because He is healing you*". Well... she didn't know me, she didn't know the problem I was going through, so that somehow touched me; and truly after that day I felt no more pain in the stomach. And I continued going to the meetings... It was amazing to see the things they spoke being fulfilled from one week to another. The result of listening to so many testimonies was the increase in my faith towards this '*Gospel*', which had just recently been presented to me.

Around the fifth meeting Gabriel gave a study talking about the 'rights' and benefits we have with the death of Jesus, which included among other things physical healing. On this day, even though I didn't know much about the Bible and prayer, I tried to put it into practice. Before going to sleep I prayed (*whatever way I knew how*), I just asked God to heal my hands in Jesus name; and to my own astonishment when I woke up the next day, I no longer felt pain in my hands! In that very moment I decided to leave behind all other beliefs I have had and follow Christ.

Introduction

God is dealing with me in His Word and challenging me in this: If I say *"I'm a follower of Christ"* and I believe the Bible is the true Word of God, why don't I act accordingly to what it says? What excuses do I give to justify my lack of faith in His Word and my lack of love?

I personally have a rational, methodical way of thinking and this book reflects the way God is helping me to 'reason' my faith (*although it may seems contradictory*) and, consequently, how it affects the way I should act in faith and in love toward others to fulfill God's commandments.

I'll approach the "healing" aspect of faith using our best and perfect example of Jesus and compare with some teachings I've been exposed to through the years in church to find if they are biblically correct or if they distort the New Covenant, which we are under.

I know I don't have enough wisdom to give you all the answers (*otherwise I'd be God*) but I'll present you some things that may challenge teachings you have learned, especially if you were raised in the church, and it is up to you to search His Word through the leading of the Spirit of God to find out truth.

One of the most important things we need to keep in our minds is that **we cannot judge the Word of God by our experiences, but judge our experiences through the Word of God**. We **cannot** create teachings that go against God's truth and against His promises. If God's truth says *"Believers shall lay hands on the sick and they shall recover"* and we don't see this manifested in our Christian life, we **cannot** doubt God's truth but we need to check our relationship with God, our intimacy with the Holy Spirit, our faith to believe God's Word, to obey it and to put it into practice.

John 6:63
It is the Spirit that gives life; the flesh profits nothing: the **words** that I speak unto you, they are S**pirit**, and they are **life**.

Matthew 4:4
But He [Jesus] answered and said, it is written, man shall not live by bread alone, but by every **word** that proceeds out of the mouth of God.

I pray that as you read this book the truth of the Word of God will become alive inside of you, stirring up faith and manifesting the amazing power of the Holy Spirit who dwells in each believer.

As we begin meditate on these questions:

Are we willing to grow in the Lord? Are we willing to change beliefs, teachings and traditions we have learned since childhood if they are contrary to the Word of God? Are we really willing to seek the Holy Spirit with all our heart and soul?

What is the motivation behind our desire to be used in healing? Is it just for people to be numbers in our list of successful healings? To exalt ourselves? To define who we are in Christ?

So with no more delays let's begin!

Am I Acting In Faith?

- Did Jesus ever lie? ☐ Yes   ☐ No

If your answer was 'No' you should agree (by faith) that **John 14:12** is true:

"Truly, truly, I say to you, he that **believes** [*have faith in*] on Me **the works that I do shall he do also**; and **greater works** than these shall he do; because I go to my Father."

Jesus purposely emphasized the word 'truly' (verily) due to the importance of what He was about to say, and because He knew many would doubt it.

Again, if your answer was 'No' you should agree that **Luke 10:19-20** is also true:

"***Behold*** I give to you **power** [*authority*] to tread on serpents and scorpions, and over **all the power of the enemy**: and *nothing* shall by any means hurt you."

Meditate on the importance of these two verses as promises of God given to us through the Holy Spirit. Does our Christian life reflect '*greater works*' (or at least the same works of Jesus) and '*authority over all power of the enemy*'?

- If it doesn't, where do you think the problem is?

    ☐ In the Word of God   ☐ In us

I don't say this to condemn anyone, because we all are growing in the knowledge of Him and in revelation of His Word, or at least we should be; but my point is that if we really believe the Bible as the true Word of God, our failure to manifest what it promises to us does **not** invalidate or discredit its truthfulness.

We need to realize that our free will has the power to limit God in the same way a Christian can quench the Holy Spirit, and stop His blessings from being received. The best example is how the Israelites wandered in the wilderness for forty years due to disobedience and unbelief.

Psalms 78:41
Yes, they turned back and tempted [tested] God, and limited the Holy One of Israel.

Revelation 3:20 says: *"Behold, I stand at the door, and knock: if any man hear My voice, and open the door, I will come in to him, and will sup with him, and he with Me"*. For me this is such a beautiful verse that shows God's goodness and grace since **He** is the one coming to our door, **He** is the one knocking, **He** is the one speaking, calling us. He does all of this out of His love for us but it is still up to us to open the door, He won't pick the lock and force entry, neither will He kick it down. Hearing Jesus' voice presupposes that He is speaking, and if He is speaking, *words* are coming out of His mouth. Are we willing to accept his *Words*? Are we willing to be His sheep, who hears His voice [*his Words*] and follow Him?

John 10:27
My sheep hear My voice, and I know them, and they follow Me.

When meditating about *'Am I acting in faith?'* three other questions come up that are of utmost importance:

- Do I believe physical healing is part of Christ's atonement?

  Isaiah 53:4-5
  Surely He took up our infirmities and carried our sorrows, yet we considered Him stricken by God, smitten by Him, and afflicted. But He was pierced for our transgressions, He was crushed for our iniquities; the punishment that brought us peace was upon Him, and by His wounds we are healed.

- Do I believe it is God's will to heal all diseases?

  Psalms 103:2-4
  *Praise the LORD, O my soul, and forget not **all His benefits** who forgives all your sins and heals **all your diseases**, who redeems your life from the pit and crowns you with love and compassion.*

- Do I really care about people dying without receiving ***all the benefits*** of the sacrifice of Jesus?

When talking about 'acting in faith' it is important to remind ourselves that actions by themselves will **not** produce faith, but actions are an important expression **of** faith. The book of James in chapter 1 verse 22 warns that those who are not doers of the Word, but only hearers, are deceived, they are reasoning contrary to truth in a misleading way. James chapter 2 also emphasizes the importance of the works of faith and even gives the analogy that *'As the body without the spirit is dead, so faith without deeds is dead'*.

Later on in this book we will dig deeper into topics that are specifically related to our beliefs about healing, but now it is necessary to address two important foundations: **The Kingdom of God** and **God's Sovereignty**. Also I will be referring to the term *'gifts of the Spirit'* as **gracings** since it comes from the Greek word

5486 *xárisma* (from "grace," **5485** */xáris*): the operation of *grace* (divine *favor*), i.e., a *grace-endowment* to edify the church.

5486 *xárisma* (grace-gift): divinely empowers a believer to share God's work with others, i.e., *Spirit-empowered service* to the church to *carry out His plan for His people*; a **free** gift of divine grace, a favor which one receives without any merit of his own.

The Kingdom Of God

What is the kingdom of God? Is it the new heaven and the new earth described in Revelation 21? Is it a governmental kingdom that will rule over the earth? Is it something we're still waiting for? Something for the future? Is it available for the believer now?

The expression *'kingdom of God'* is not only about the rule of an eternal sovereign God over all creation as mentioned in **Psalm 103:19** and **Daniel 4:3**, it also relates to the new birth [*from above*] described in **John 3:3-7** in Jesus' interaction with Nicodemus:

*"Jesus answered and said to him, truly, truly, I say to you, except a man be born again, he cannot see the kingdom of God. Nicodemus said to Him, how can a man be born when he is old? Can he enter the second time into his mother's womb, and be born? Jesus answered, truly, truly, I say to you, except a man be **born of water** and **of the Spirit**, he cannot enter into the kingdom of God. That which is born of the flesh is flesh; and that which is born of the Spirit is spirit. Marvel not that I said to you, you must be born again [from above]"*.

Jesus said in **Matthew 6:10** (Luke 11) when one his disciples asked Him to teach [impart knowledge] them to pray: *"...Your kingdom* come. Your will be done, as in heaven, so in earth"*.

* from the Greek [932] *basileía*: kingdom, sovereignty, royal power. The realm in which a king sovereignly rules. Also refers to the rule of Christ in the hearts of believers.

So let's see other passages and the context in which this same word [932] *basileía* [kingdom] is used, and meditate on what they relate to:

John 18:36
Jesus answered, **My kingdom is not of this world**: if My kingdom were of this world, then would My servants fight, that I should not be delivered to the Jews: but now is My kingdom not from hence.

Luke 17:21
And when He was demanded of the Pharisees, when the kingdom of God should come, He answered them and said, **the kingdom of God comes not with observation** [*signs to be observed*]: Neither shall they say, **see** here! Or, **see** there! For, behold, **the kingdom of God is within you**.

The Jews believed and expected for the manifestation of the '*kingdom of God*', but for them it meant God sending them a leader to overtake the Roman dominion, restore them as an independent nation and rule the Earth. But Jesus explained that their view of kingdom of God was erroneous, it was not a '*kingdom*' as they knew - a form of government, as we can see also in the following passages:

Mark 1:14-15
Jesus came into Galilee, preaching the gospel of the kingdom of God, and saying, **the time is fulfilled** [*complete*], and **the kingdom of God is at hand**: repent you, and believe the gospel.

Matthew 10:7-8
And as you go, preach, saying, the kingdom of heaven is at hand [has drawn *near*]. Heal the sick, cleanse the lepers, raise the dead, cast out devils: freely you have received, freely give.

Mark 10:15
Truly I say to you, whoever shall not receive the kingdom of God as a little child, he shall not enter therein.

Mark 4:11
And He said to them, to you it is given to know the mystery [*is not something unknowable, rather, it is what can only be known through revelation*] of the kingdom of God: but to them that are without [*revelation*], all these things are done in parables.

Romans 14:17
For the **kingdom of God** is not meat and drink; but righteousness [*of which God is the author*], and peace [*wholeness*], and joy [*awareness of God's grace*] **in the Holy Ghost** [*Spirit*].

1 Corinthians 4:20
For the kingdom of God is not in word, but in **power**.

Mark 9:1
And He said to them, truly I say to you, that there be some of them that stand here, which shall not taste of death, till they have seen **the kingdom of God come with power.**

Acts 1:8
But you shall receive **power**, after that the **Holy Ghost** is come on you:

Matthew 12:28
But if I cast out devils by the **Spirit of God**, then **the kingdom of God is come to you**.

Nowadays some Christians are also passively waiting for their '*kingdom of God*', for Jesus to come back to rescue them from this *evil* world so He can take away their sufferings and they can be in the presence of God. Yes, the book of Revelation also describes an eternal kingdom, the "New Jerusalem", as the final inheritance. But what was the kingdom Jesus was referring to?

According to Jesus' words let's see what the kingdom of God is **not**:

- The kingdom of God is **not** something to be perceived through the natural eyes, something 'exterior' that can be identified by sight.

- The kingdom of God is **not** something for the future, something that is to come, as Jesus said '*the time was fulfilled, the kingdom of God was at hand*', it is a present reality.

The **kingdom** to which Jesus referred was from a different nature, a kingdom that not only had already come, but could (*can*) be entered in, which presence was (*is*) manifested by the **power** of the **Holy Spirit** through the life of those who were **born from above**. And because this kingdom has come, the sick can be healed, the lepers cleansed, the dead raised and the devils casted out.

Matthew 6:33
But seek [*desire, search*] you first the **kingdom of God**, and **His** righteousness (*not ours*); and all these things [*earthly needs*] shall be added to you.

God's Sovereignty

To say God is in control of everything but at the same time say man has free will is a logical impossibility. God can work anything that happens for His good, but that does not mean that everything that happens is His will or that He was the one who caused it in the first place; otherwise you would say that 'sin' is His will, because *'He allows'* it to happen.

One of the biggest deceptions in the church today is the one concerning God's sovereignty; and our misunderstanding of it will **directly** and **greatly** affect how we perceive and receive from Him through faith.

First of all, it is necessary for us to acknowledge that there are no actual words 'sovereign' or 'sovereignty' from the original Hebrew or Greek in the Bible; we can't find them in translations like the old King James Version [KJV] and the English Standard Version [ESV]. We only find them in the two main newer translations: New International Version [NIV] and New Living Translation [NLT]. In the Old Testament we see the Hebrew words [136]**adonay** [lord/master] and [3069]**Yahweh** [God] coupled forming the expression we know as '**Lord God**' being translated in the NIV and NLT as '**sovereign Lord**'. In the New Testament we see the Greek word [1203] **despótēs** translated as **lord** or **master** being translated in the NIV and NLT also as '**sovereign Lord**'.

There is no problem for us to use the word 'sovereign' as an adjective to God **if** we use the dictionary definition of it, which is: having supreme rank, power or authority; preeminent, indisputable; greatest in degree; above all others in character, importance and excellence; efficacious, potent. The deception lies in the definition **religion** created for the word 'sovereign'; teaching as if God being sovereign means: "*He has the control of all things! Nothing can happen without first having His approval, without Him allowing; because in the end of it all nothing can happen against His ultimate will!*"

You might (wrongly) say, "*Well if God allowed this to happen to me, it is because He has a purpose*". In other words, "*If God allowed Satan to touch me, is because it is God's desire that I go through this*". Well if you think this way, you are calling God a liar. Let me show you why: If I follow this wrong thinking about God's sovereignty where He controls everything, I can (wrongly) conclude that "*If God allowed Adam and Eve to eat from the tree of the knowledge of good and evil, it was because it was His desire for them to eat*". But that would make God a liar since He was the one who commanded them not to eat the fruit in the first place.

By this wrong concept of God's sovereignty, I can (wrongly) say, "*So if it is God's desire for all men to be saved* (**1 Timothy 2:4**), *that will happen! Nobody will ever go to hell*". Anyone who believes that people who reject Christ will be condemned to hell by default **cannot** (should not) believe that God controls **all** things according to His will, because if He did, no one would be condemned. **Unless we have a deep understanding of how our God-given gift of free will impacts God's own will to our lives, our 'Christian experience' as believers will be rooted in a flimsy and unstable foundation.**

If God is using Satan to do His will in our lives, whom should we pray to? Why would we even pray? The only thing left for us would be to accept whatever happens to us, because "*if He allowed it, then surely it is His will!*".

As Bill Johnson says: Why would God raise something up to be His will that He empowers us to pray against?

Another polemic question related to God's sovereignty is:

"Is God the one who decides the time of our death?"

Deuteronomy 30:19
I call heaven and earth to record this day against you, that I have set before you life and death, blessing and cursing: therefore choose life, that both you and your seed may live.

If God was the one controlling '*all*' things, including the exact time that we die, why would He command **us** to choose life instead of death?

From God's perspective, because He is omniscient, He knows everything and knows exactly when, where and how we will die. Nothing we can do will change what God already knows will happen. However, that does not mean that was the time and the way God intended for us. Obviously, a person who commits suicide causes his own death, and certainly, it is not God's desire that any die this way. The fact that God has a specific plan for our lives laid out before we even existed doesn't mean that it will come to pass and that we will surrender our lives to Him in order to fulfill it.

From our perspective, what we do has an impact on when, where, and how we die; otherwise why would we even bother seeking medical assistance or praying for healing? We would leave everything 'up to God'. A simple meditation on God's commandment "*Honor your father and mother; which is the first commandment with promise; that it may be well with you, and you may live long on the earth*" shows a conditional promise. It depends on our part (not God's) to decide to live more or less days on the earth according to the way we act.

Let's now reflect on God's sovereignty related to physical healing. The New Testament shows innumerous stories of people who strived after Jesus for their healings; people like the woman with the issue of blood, the paralyzed man who was carried and lowered through the roof by four men, the two blind men who didn't quit shouting even with the crowd's opposition.

What would have happened to them if they had quit half way? If they had lost hope half way? If they had lost faith half way? They would not have received their healing and God's sovereignty would have nothing to do with that!

God desired all of them to be healed. But if any of them for any reason had stopped believing Jesus had the power to heal, or started doubting Jesus' willingness to heal or even quit because they were more worried about men's opinion about them, they would not have received the blessing (healing) of God.

Many Christians use the kind of concept of God's sovereignty in which He controls everything as an excuse to make them feel comfortable and justified when they do not get the results the Bible promises they should have. They prefer to blame God rather than hold themselves accountable for their lack of communion with the Holy Spirit.

Jesus performed all the miracles, signs and wonders not as God, but as a man of flesh and blood (*like you and me*) surrendered to the Holy Spirit. **Perfect communion with the Holy Spirit leads to perfect results. That is why Jesus never failed to heal a single person — Love never fails.**

Galatians 5:6
For in Jesus Christ neither circumcision avails anything, nor uncircumcision; but **faith which works by love**.

1 Peter 4:8
And above all things have fervent charity [*love*] among yourselves: for charity [*love*] shall cover the multitude of sins.

The Word of God warns us that it is even possible to manifest faith apart from love, but the results of a 'loveless' faith can be read as follows:

Matthew 7:21-23
Not every one that said to Me, Lord, Lord, shall enter into the kingdom of heaven; but he that does the will of my Father which is in heaven. Many will say to Me in that day, Lord, Lord, have we not prophesied in Your name? And in Your name have cast out devils? And in Your name done many wonderful works? And then will I profess to them, I never knew you: depart from Me, you that work iniquity.

1 Corinthians 13:2
And though I have the gift of prophecy, and understand all mysteries, and all knowledge; and though I have all faith, so that I could remove mountains, and have not charity [love], I am nothing.

If we are not producing Christ-like works we might need a greater revelation of God's love. By this I mean a greater revelation of His love manifested towards us in form of God's **grace** and **mercy,** a greater revelation of God's love which is manifested through Christ's crucifixion and sacrifice that made us the **righteousness** of God in Him (**2 Corinthians 5:21**), a greater revelation of God's love which makes us **sons of God (1 John 3:1)**, so that we can approach the throne of God with **confidence** and **boldness (Hebrews 4:16)**.

Suffering For Being A Christian

I am sure most people heard this in church: "*This person is going through this disease to be an example to others*", as if diseases were the sufferings, trials and tribulations that Christians must go through.

Well if that is true, why did Jesus heal all those who came to him?

1 Peter 4:12-15
Dear friends, do not be surprised at the **painful trial** you are suffering, as though something strange were happening to you. But rejoice that you participate in the **sufferings of Christ**, so that you may be overjoyed when His glory is revealed. If you are insulted because of the name of Christ, you are blessed, for the Spirit of glory and of God rests on you. If you suffer, it should not be as a murderer or thief or any other kind of criminal, or even as a meddler. However, if you **suffer as a Christian**, do not be ashamed, but praise God that you bear that name.

In the beatitudes, Jesus **never** said, "*blessed are those who are sick and have diseases...*" He said in **Matthew 5:10-12**:

"*Blessed are those who are **persecuted** because of righteousness, for theirs is the kingdom of heaven. Blessed are you when people **insult you, persecute you and falsely say all kinds of evil against you because of Me**. Rejoice and be glad, because great is your reward in heaven, for in the same way they persecuted the prophets who were before you*".

- Is there any place in the Bible that says that Jesus was sick or had any disease? ☐ Yes ☐ No

- Why would some people say of Christ's sufferings, trial and tribulation, that it was a possible *sickness or diseases?*

The sufferings of Christ cannot be diseases by the simple fact that when you are sick you cannot fulfill God's commandment to *"go preach the gospel"*.

One verse you could try to argue to justify a disease as being God's will to a person is **John 9:3-4**:

"Jesus answered, neither has this man sinned, nor his parents: *but [however / nevertheless / on the other hand]* that the **works of God** should be **made manifest** *[known / visible]* in him. I **must** *[what is absolutely necessary]* work the **works** of Him that sent Me, while it is day: the night comes, when no man can work".

Well before you blame God for the man's blindness since birth, consider: Jesus said twice in this passage about the "works of God", what was it? Was it blindness? No! Jesus was not talking about blindness as a work of God, but that was absolutely necessary that should be made known God's work in that person, that is, displaying the will of God by restoring the man's eyesight. Meditate on these two verses:

Romans 5:12
Why, as by one man sin entered into the world, and death by sin; and so death passed on all men, for that all have sinned.

Romans 3:10 & 23
As it is written, there is none righteous, no, not one.
For all have sinned, and come short of the glory of God;

When Jesus said, *"neither has this man sinned nor his parents"* He was not saying that the man had never sinned in his life, but that the sins he had committed was not a direct cause of the blindness

- it seems obvious because he was blind from birth, unless he had sinned inside his mother's womb, that I don't think it is reasonable to speculate.

The effects of sin, with the fall of man, have ramifications not only with the spiritual death, but with entrance of sickness, aging and bodily death into the Earth, including diseases caused by mutation of DNA. All these things were never God's intent for mankind.

Be careful! **John 9:3-4** does not say that God made the man blind, on purpose, so He could heal him - otherwise God would be the one inoculating poison and administering the antidote at the same time. I believe it simply says that although the man (*as all of us*) was born in a "fallen world" and was blind from birth, God in that very moment would manifest His works in him. So if you still want to justify suffering with diseases, next time you meet a blind person from birth, you, as a representative of Christ, should do the same thing that Christ did, set the person free and heal him.

This episode is just one among others, as we will see later in this study, where the person did not know who Jesus was, never went to Him, never asked to be healed; Jesus was the one who saw the person, went to him, had compassion and healed.

Unfortunately, many Christians say wrong things like, "*God allowed this disease so I could know Him*", as if the disease was a blessing from God instead of a curse from sin; or "*Through this sickness I was able to preach the gospel to the doctor and nurses*", as if God made the person sick so he or she could preach the gospel at the hospital. We need to be careful to put things in the right perspective, reflect on these three important statements:

- Everything that happens is known by God, but not everything that happens is God's will;

- Not everything that is 'allowed' by God is His will (e.g., sin).

- God can turn around anything that happens for good as it says in **Romans 8:28**, but it does not mean that it was His will or His purpose for it to happen in first place.

It is important to highlight that this passage of John 9, as well as the forgiven thief on the cross, destroy the concept of karma present in some religions.

Paul's Thorn In The Flesh

This is the next thing we are taught when talking about sickness and diseases.

Is there anything that indicates Paul's thorn in the flesh as a disease?

2 Corinthians 12:7-10
To keep me from becoming conceited because of these surpassing great revelations, there was given me a thorn in my flesh, a **messenger*1 of Satan**, to **torment*2** me. Three times I pleaded with the Lord to take it away from me. **And*3** He said to me, "My grace [*favor*] is **sufficient*4** for you, for My power is **made perfect*5** in weakness." Therefore I will boast all the more gladly about my weaknesses, so that Christ's power may **rest*6** on me. That is why, for Christ's sake, I delight in **weaknesses**, in **insults**, in **hardships**, in **persecutions**, in **difficulties**. For when I am weak, then I am strong.

This is how 'traditional teaching' reads this passage: "*God gave Paul a thorn in his flesh, probably a sickness or disease, to keep him humble, and even though he pleaded three times God still didn't take it away from him...*". But is that really what the Bible says about it?

Let's go back and meditate carefully on this passage considering the Greek meaning of each of the following words in the context:

*1 from the Greek 32 *aggelos*: **angel, messenger or delegate either human or heavenly.**

*2 from the Greek ²⁸⁵² *kolaphizē*: **strike with the fist, buffet; mistreat violently.**

*3 from the Greek ²⁵³² *kai*:   **and, even, also, namely.** Some translations use "but" instead of "and" - that is a huge mistake because "*kai*" is *never* adversative [expressing opposition], it *never* means "however", "but". Most people read this passage of 2 Corinthians as if Paul asked God something *but* He denied his request. As the Strong's reference says, the word ²⁵³² *kai* does **not** express opposition. Because of this we cannot conclude that God denied Paul's request, but we should read as it is written, that means: Paul called upon God three times *and* He said...

*4 from the Greek ⁷¹⁴ *arkeó*: **to assist, suffice;** to be possessed of unfailing strength; to be strong, to be enough (as against any danger; hence, to defend, ward off).

*5 from the Greek ⁵⁰⁵⁵ *teleó*: **end, finish, fulfill, accomplish, complete, consummate, perform, execute;**

*6 from the Greek ¹⁹⁸¹ *episkénoó*: **raise a tent (over), dwell;** of the power of Christ descending upon one, working within him and giving him help.

So rewriting this passage with the meanings described above we can read it as:

2 Corinthians 12:7-10 *(with my commentaries between parentheses)*
To keep me from becoming **haughty** because of these surpassingly *(Godly)* great revelations, there was given me a thorn *(affliction)* in my flesh [carnal part not transformed by God], *(which was inflicted by)* a messenger of Satan, to **mistreat** me **violently.** Three times I **called upon** the Lord to take it away from me **and** He said to me, "My **unmerited favor, which is always leaning toward you, is of unfailing strength to defend you**

32

against any danger, for My power is **performed** when **you are without strength** *(not relying on carnal self-confidence)*". Therefore, I will boast all the more gladly **when I lack strength** *(in my carnal self)*, so that Christ's power *(Spirit-confidence)* may **abide** in me. That is why, for Christ's sake, I delight in weaknesses, in insults, in hardships, in persecutions, in difficulties. For when I am **without strength** *(not relying on carnal self-confidence)*, then I am **empowered** *(trust in God's grace and power to be manifested in my life through His Spirit who abides in me)*.

How many of us have difficulties hearing the voice of God? How many of us seek God for an answer but are not sure of what His answer is? Isn't it amazing that concerning this 'affliction' Paul needed to call upon God *(only)* 3 times to be able to hear clearly from God? I don't see the fact that Paul needed to persist 3 times as the unwillingness of God to answer him in the first 2 times; but I see Paul's need to focus on God in order to be sensitive to His voice and in this instance as scriptures state, it took him 3 times. Not bad!

The truth is:

- 'Thorn in the flesh' is an expression that doesn't necessarily mean something physical (in his body), the same way we use the expression 'pain in the neck' for something or someone that causes us trouble or affliction.

- God never gave Paul the 'thorn'. Satan did it through his messenger to mistreat Paul with violence through insults, hardships, persecutions and to make him stop doing God's works, i.e., undo the works of Satan. Does it make any sense that God would give Paul something to hinder him from doing God's own work?

- When God answered Paul, it was not to justify why He would not help him. But it was to reinforce that when we can't overcome a situation in our own strength or ability, the power of God is like a 'tent' over us, present and ready to accomplish His promises that He will never leave us nor forsake us, providing the supernatural resources necessary to meet all our needs according to His riches in glory in Christ Jesus.

- Even if you *somehow* decided to believe that Paul's thorn was a disease, the reason Paul gave for him to receive this 'thorn' (*from Satan*) was the **abundance of the revelation**. So if you are not receiving *abundant revelation* as Paul received, you **cannot** put yourself in his place.

There are two ways to read "My grace [*favor*] is sufficient for you":

The first one is the 'unmerciful way' as if God answered Paul like that: "Paul stop asking for this! It is not my desire to help you! You should be glad that I already gave you the grace to go to heaven one day! Stop bugging me!" Unfortunately, most Christians understand and teach this passage like that.

The second one reads like: "Yes Paul, there is nothing greater than My grace and My favor toward you. My grace is sufficient to destroy all the arrows of the enemy against your life. Don't worry, whenever you face a situation in which you feel weak and helpless, stop relying on yourself, on your own strength and ability and start relying on Me, on My Spirit, on My grace and My power will be manifested to give you the victory"

I don't know about you, but as I read this passage in the light of the Greek as demonstrated previously, I perceive a slight (*not to say huge*) different meaning from the 'traditional' way of understanding it. Instead of this passage being understood as a hopeless situation for Paul where God did not care about his situation, I see just the opposite, as an encouraging scripture in which God redirects Paul not to trust in himself and in his own strength, but to put his trust in Him so His grace could be manifested on his behalf.

It is up to us to choose, which *'kind of god'* we put our faith in: a condemning and hard-hearted *god*, or a merciful, caring and loving God.

There is no reference in the Bible to support the teaching of Paul's thorn as possibly being a disease, even because when we go to the Greek it is more likely that means physical aggression than any other possibility. Note that right before this passage of 2 Corinthians 12:7-10, Paul also talks about his sufferings in **2 Corinthians 11: 23-29** as the insults, beatings and hardships he went through for the sake of Christ:

"Are they ministers of Christ? (I speak as a fool) I am more; in labors more abundant, in stripes above measure, in prisons more frequent, in deaths oft. Of the Jews five times received I forty stripes save one. Thrice was I beaten with rods, once was I stoned, thrice I suffered shipwreck, a night and a day I have been in the deep; in journeys often, in perils of waters, in perils of robbers, in perils by my own countrymen, in perils by the heathen, in perils in the city, in perils in the wilderness, in perils in the sea, in perils among false brothers; In weariness and painfulness, in watchings often, in hunger and thirst, in fastings often, in cold and nakedness. Beside those things that are without, that which comes on me daily, the care of all the churches. Who is weak, and I am not weak? who is offended, and I burn not?"

Whatever we believe from the Word of God is what we will receive from it, in other words, if we believe that God allows sickness and disease as a way to teach us something or to bring us close to him, guess what? We are the one giving the enemy authority to harm us! That's why God warned in **Hosea 4:6**: "*My people perish for lack of knowledge*".

If we stand firm in the Word of God, submitting the renewing of our mind through God's truth and resisting the enemy's lies, he will flee from us. (**Romans 12:2** and **James 4:7**)

Did Jesus Ever Deny Healing Anyone?
The Effects Of Faith

In the biblical accounts, there is just one passage where someone came to Jesus asking for healing and, at first, He denied it. Let's read this account as described in Mark and Matthew:

Mark 7:25-30
For a certain woman, whose young daughter had an unclean spirit, heard of Him, and came and fell at His feet: The woman was a Greek, a Syrophenician by nation; and she sought Him that He would cast forth the devil out of her daughter. But Jesus said to her, **let the children first be filled: for it is not meet to take the children's bread, and to cast it to the dogs**. And she answered and said to Him, yes, Lord: yet the dogs under the table eat of the children's crumbs. And He said to her, **for this saying go your way**; the devil is gone out of your daughter. And when she was come to her house, she found the devil gone out, and her daughter laid on the bed.

Matthew 15:21-28
Then Jesus went there, and departed into the coasts of Tyre and Sidon. And, behold, a woman of Canaan came out of the same coasts, and cried to Him, saying, have mercy on me, o Lord, You son of David; my daughter is grievously vexed with a devil. **But He answered her not a word**. And His disciples came and sought Him, saying, send her away; for she cries after us. But He answered and said, **I am not sent but to the lost sheep of the house of Israel**. Then came she and worshipped Him, saying, Lord, help me. But He answered and said, **it is not meet to take the children's bread, and to cast it to dogs**. And she said, truth,

Lord: yet the dogs eat of the crumbs which fall from their masters' table. Then Jesus answered and said to her, **o woman, great is your faith: be it to you even as you will**. And her daughter was made whole from that very hour.

Before creating a rule of Jesus' unwillingness to heal for today, we must consider that in the chronology of Jesus' ministry his focus was first for the Jewish as He mentioned in his own words *"I am not sent but to the lost sheep of the house of Israel"*. We also can see this previously mentioned in **Matthew 10:5-6** when He commissioned the disciples:

"These twelve Jesus sent forth, and commanded them, saying, Go not into the way of the Gentiles, and into any city of the Samaritans enter you not: But go rather to the lost sheep of the house of Israel".

Although His primary purpose was to reach first the Jewish, Jesus pointed out to a change of attitude [heart] towards the Samaritans, as when He passed through their town and interacted not only with the woman at the well, but with all those who listened to her testimony and came to Him, as can be read in **John 4:1-42**. Another important reference is the parable of the good Samaritan in **Luke 10:25-37**.

In the end of the gospel of Matthew and in the beginning of Acts, Jesus himself commissioned the apostles to go to all nations, as we read below:

Matthew 28:18-20
And Jesus came and spoke to them, saying, all power is given to Me in heaven and in earth. Go you therefore, and teach **all nations**, baptizing them in the name of the Father, and of the Son, and of the Holy Ghost: Teaching them to observe all things whatever I have commanded you: and, see, I am with you always, even to the end of the world. Amen.

Acts 1:8
But you shall receive power, after that the Holy Ghost is come on you: and you shall be witnesses to Me both in Jerusalem, and in all Judaea, and in Samaria, and to the uttermost part of the earth.

The great persecution in Jerusalem was an important factor that influenced the spread of the gospel throughout Judea and Samaria, as mentioned in **Acts 8** through Philip, Peter and John. We see the gospel being preached to the gentiles at Cornelius' house as in **Acts 10**. Paul also acknowledged the impartiality of the gospel as in **Romans 1:16-17**:

"For I am not ashamed of the gospel of Christ: for it is the power of God to salvation to everyone that believes; to the Jew first, and also to the Greek. For therein is the righteousness of God revealed from faith to faith: as it is written, the just shall live by faith".

So returning to our main verses of **Mark 7:25-30** and **Matthew 15:21-28**, what can we conclude about God's desire concerning healing from this passage? Yes, it is His desire to heal everyone: Jews, Samaritans, and gentiles. I believe the most important lesson is that even though it was not time for Jesus to minister to the gentiles, the expression of **her** faith was rewarded by God, to the point of Jesus acknowledging her as having *great* faith and granting her petition. This is a great example for what the Bible says in **Hebrews 11:6**:

*"But without faith it is impossible to please Him: for he that comes to God must believe that He is, and that **He is a rewarder of them that diligently seek Him.**"*

Are we diligently seeking God?

Are we persistently renewing our mind according to His Word to be able to prove what is that good, and acceptable, and perfect, will of God?

The other example of great faith acknowledged by Jesus in the New Testament is in **Matthew 8:5-13** (Luke 7:1-10):

"And when Jesus was entered into Capernaum, there came to Him a centurion, beseeching Him, and saying, Lord, my servant lies at home sick of the palsy, grievously tormented. And **Jesus said to him, I will come and heal him.** *The centurion answered and said, Lord, I am not worthy that You should come under my roof:* **but speak the word only, and my servant shall be healed.** *For I am a man under authority, having soldiers under me: and I say to this man, go, and he goes; and to another, come, and he comes; and to my servant, do this, and he does it.* **When Jesus heard it, He marveled,** *and said to them that followed,* **truly I say to you, I have not found so great faith, no, not in Israel.** *And I say to you, that many shall come from the east and west, and shall sit down with Abraham, and Isaac, and Jacob, in the kingdom of heaven. But the children of the kingdom shall be cast out into outer darkness: there shall be weeping and gnashing of teeth. And Jesus said to the centurion,* **go your way; and as you have believed, so be it done to you.** *And his servant was healed in the selfsame hour."*

What amazes me in this passage is the fact that even though Jesus said *"I will come and heal him"*, the centurion presented such faith and understanding of Jesus' authority that he would turn to Jesus and say something along the lines of *"You don't need to go there and lay your hands on him, just a word from your mouth and he will be healed"*. This is another great example of how the expression of our faith pleases God.

Does God Pick And Choose
Who He Wants To Heal?

Many Christians say the phrase *'God is sovereign'* in the context of healing, in a way as if they couldn't know if it is God's desire to heal a person. But what do the Bible and Jesus' example really teach us?

If we don't know God's will, how can we be confident to approach and ask anything of God? If we are not confident in approaching God, can we really manifest "true" faith? If we don't have faith and act in it, can we please God?

If it was God's desire that people be sick and have diseases why would He promise that if we lay hands on the sick they would be healed? Wouldn't God be contradicting Himself?

Where does the *"pick and choose"* teaching comes from?

It comes from the healing at the pool of Bethesda in **John 5:1-17**. Let's read this passage: "*After these things there was a feast of the Jews, and Jesus went up to Jerusalem. Now there is in Jerusalem by the sheep gate a pool, which is called in Hebrew Bethesda, having five porticoes. In these lay a multitude of those who were sick, blind, lame, and withered, waiting for the moving of the waters; for an angel of the Lord went down at certain seasons into the pool and stirred up the water; whoever then first, after the stirring up of the water, stepped in was made well from whatever disease with which he was afflicted. A man was there who had been ill for thirty-eight years. When Jesus saw him lying there, and knew that he had already been a long time in that condition, He said to him, "Do you wish to get well?" The sick man* answered Him, "Sir, I have no man to put me into the pool when the water is stirred up, but while I am coming, another steps down before me." Jesus said to him, "Get up, pick up your pallet and walk." Immediately the man became well, and picked up his pallet and began to walk.

Now it was the Sabbath on that day. So the Jews were saying to the man who was cured, "It is the Sabbath, and it is not permissible for you to carry your pallet." But he answered them, "He who made me well was the one who said to me, 'Pick up your pallet and walk.'" They asked him, "Who is the man who said to you, 'Pick up your pallet and walk'?" But the man who was healed did not know who it was, for Jesus had slipped away while there was a crowd in that place. Afterward Jesus found him in the temple and said to him, "Behold, you have become well; do not sin anymore, so that nothing worse happens to you." The man went away, and told the Jews that it was Jesus who had made him well. For this reason the Jews were persecuting Jesus, because He was doing these things on the Sabbath. But He answered them, "My Father is working until now, and I Myself am working."

Many Christians interpret this passage like this: "*Did you see? Jesus went to a place where there was a bunch of sick people but He healed just one! So it is not God's will to heal every person.*" If you believe in the "*pick and choose*" teaching, meditate on these three points:

- Yes, **John 5:1-17** is an account of the healing of one man, but is there anything in the Bible affirming that Jesus didn't heal any other person on that place before or after that man's healing? Doesn't the same gospel of John say on the last verse *"And there are also many other things which Jesus did, which if they were written in detail, I suppose that even the world itself would not contain the books that would be written"*?

- Even if Jesus only healed that one man, doesn't **John 5:17** say that the Jews were persecuting Him because He was healing on the Sabbath? So couldn't it be the reason why He didn't heal other people? They were trying to seize Him but His time had not yet come, so He had to leave that place? But if Jesus didn't have the opportunity and time to heal all other people in the pool of Bethesda due to persecution, does it mean that it was not God's desire to heal them all?

• Did Jesus heal and preach to every person on planet Earth in His three-year ministry period? Of course not. Geographical factors had influences. For example, Jesus didn't heal any person in North or South America. Does it mean that is not God's desire that people be healed and the gospel be preached in these continents?

Concerning this, Jesus said in **Luke 4:43**: "*I must preach the good news of the kingdom of God to the other towns also, because that is why I was sent.*" So by this we see a possibility of people that may not have had the chance to go to Jesus to be healed, because He couldn't stay still in just one city. Does it mean that it was not God's desire to heal them all?

So if we can't add to the Word of God, we need to see it for what it says and not create doctrines from what it doesn't say, i.e., manmade teachings.

Tradition comes and says: "*...well God is sovereign...*" making implicit or explicit the following statement: "*maybe it was not God's desire to heal this person*". Unfortunately, this is commonly used and even taught by Christians to justify their experiences of when they prayed for someone and the person didn't get healed, because it is easier to create a cop-out than hold themselves accountable to produce the results that the Word of God promises.

We should never forget that Satan used God's own Word to try to deceive (even) Jesus. So we need to be careful **not** to put *our* doctrines and *our* own understanding of scriptures above the Truth, that is, above the person and character of Jesus.

- Imagine if Jesus appears today to a person with a terminal liver disease due to alcoholism, and this person asked Him to be healed. What do you think Jesus would do? Do you think Jesus would say:

"You are reaping what you sowed. It is your fault. I can give you salvation but I won't heal you"?

If you think that it is God's will that someone deserves to reap a sickness or disease for what they sowed in their past, wouldn't it be the same as Jesus saying to the adulterous woman: "Yes you've sinned! I will forgive you and save you but you will still reap what you sowed, so you'll be stoned to death."

Well, if we really do deserve to reap what we sowed, we should all deserve hell, shouldn't we?

Now let's read the passage about the woman with the issue of blood in **Mark 5:25-34** (Luke 8:43-48, Matthew 9:20-22):

"And a certain woman, which had an issue of blood twelve years, and had suffered many things of many physicians, and had spent all that she had, and was nothing bettered, but rather grew worse, when she had heard of Jesus, came in the press behind, and touched His garment. For she said, If I may touch but His clothes, I shall be whole. And straightway the fountain of her blood was dried up; and she fell in her body that she was healed of that plague. And Jesus, immediately knowing in himself that virtue had gone out of Him, turned him about in the press, and said, Who touched My clothes? And his disciples said to Him, You see the multitude thronging [pressing] You, and say You, who touched

me? And He looked round about to see her that had done this thing. But the woman fearing and trembling, knowing what was done in her, came and fell down before Him, and told Him all the truth. And He said to her, daughter, your faith has made you whole; go in peace, and be whole of your plague."

By reading this passage, someone could say, *"Did you see? The crowd was surrounding and touching Jesus but just one person got healed, so it is not God's will to heal everybody!"*If that is you, please read the following three passages before going any further and creating a doctrine out of this observation:

Mark 3:9-10
And He spoke to his disciples, that a small ship should wait on Him because of the multitude, lest they should throng Him.
For He had healed many [*numerous, multitudinous*]; so that they pressed on Him for to touch Him, as many as had plagues.

Matthew 14:35-36
And when the men of that place had knowledge of Him, they sent out into all that country round about, and brought to Him all that were diseased; and **sought Him that they might only touch the hem of His garment:** and **as many as touched were made perfectly whole.**

Luke 6:19
And they that were vexed with unclean spirits: and they were healed. And the whole multitude **sought to touch Him: for there went virtue out of Him, and healed them all.**

As we read above in the accounts of **Matthew 14 and Luke 6**, **everyone** (*no exceptions*) who touched Jesus was healed, that is why the multitude were after Him.

So, let us not take wrong conclusions of what is **not** written in the Word, the passage of **Mark 5** never states that the other people who touched Jesus weren't healed, neither that those people were thronging Jesus with the intent to receive healing, although in my opinion that is what they were after. **Mark 5** highlights a woman who pressed into the crowd and appropriated her healing [*Jesus' power*] through her faith.

My *personal* point of view about **Mark 5** (*you can discard it if you want*) is that it shows the same situation of **Matthew 14** and **Luke 6**, people thronging after Jesus for healing and every person being healed. The difference about the woman in **Mark 5** was the '*quality*' of faith she presented. That is why Jesus acknowledged her touch among the touch of other people. Although the crowd also 'touched' Jesus, I believe they had a kind of faith which was *co-dependent* of Jesus' faith, the kind which says: "*If You are willing, You can heal me*". That is, their healing depended on Jesus releasing His faith in order for them to actually be made whole. Meanwhile the woman had a different kind of faith, which made her appropriate healing independent of Jesus releasing power intentionally by His own actions.

No matter whether my view is true or not, the importance of having this woman's story mentioned in the Bible is to teach us four things:

- The importance of believing Jesus as the source of healing;

- The importance of acting in faith and pressing towards the 'goal' in order to receive it, instead of being passively waiting 'God' to decide it He '*wants to heal or not*';

- The importance of persisting despite the crowd [*barriers, obstacles*] or even against the 'Law', which prohibited a person with her issue (considered '*impure*') to be among other people;

- The importance of trusting God first. Unfortunately, many will only turn to God after they have tried everything the *medical world* has to offer.

Why would anyone say that God picks and chooses who He wants to heal when **Acts 10:34**, **Romans 2:11**, **Deuteronomy 10:17** and **Job 34:19** say *God does **not** show favoritism*?

Does God Want Every Person Healed?
The Effects Of Doubt

Mark 1:40-41 (Luke 5:12-15)
A man with leprosy came to Him and begged Him on his knees,
"**If You are willing**, You can make me clean." **Filled with
compassion**, Jesus reached out His hand and touched the man. "**I
am willing**," He said. "Be clean!"

Let's reflect on the phrase "*If you are willing, you can make me
clean*": Did we ever stop to think how bad is the meaning of this
phrase? The man with leprosy never doubted Jesus' power
[ability] to heal. He doubted Jesus' willingness [desire] to heal. In
other words, he said: "I know you can, but I'm not sure you want
to..."

It would be much better if he had said the opposite "*I know you
want to, but I don't know if you can*". Because by saying "*if you are
willing*" he doubted Jesus' will - Jesus' love. That's why (I believe)
Jesus was filled with compassion for the man. Because by saying
that, he showed that he didn't have an understanding of Jesus'
character and consequently of God's love.

In the following example which would be the worst attitude:

It is 6pm and a homeless person comes and asks you to buy a
lunch for him to eat because he is starving and has not eaten
anything that day.

1. You have the desire to help [love] but unfortunately, you can't
   because you really have no money [ability];

2. You have the money [ability], but you don't have the desire to
   help [love].

- **How many times did we do the same thing, doubting God's love and desire to heal?**

Matthew 17:14-21 (Mark 9:14-29; Luke 9:37-42)
And when they were come to the multitude, there came to Him a certain man, kneeling down to Him, and saying, Lord, **have mercy** on my son: for he is lunatic, and sore vexed: for often he falls into the fire, and oft into the water. And I brought him to Your disciples, and they could not cure him. Then Jesus answered and said, **o faithless and perverse generation, how long shall I be with you? how long shall I suffer you?** Bring him here to Me. And Jesus rebuked the devil; and he departed out of him: and the child was cured from that very hour. Then came the disciples to Jesus apart, and said, why could not we cast him out? And Jesus said to them, **because of your unbelief***[little faith]: for truly I say to you, If you have faith as a grain of mustard seed, you shall say to this mountain, remove hence to yonder place; and it shall remove; **and nothing shall be impossible to you**. However, this kind goes not out but by prayer and fasting.

Let's put Matthew 17 in the context of our churches nowadays:

Someone has cancer and comes to pray for healing. After the prayer, no improvement is seen for some time, and the person's situation gets worse. So we say: "*Maybe it is not God's timing to heal the person*". Then the person dies of cancer and we say "*It was not God's will to heal that person*".

The apostles could have used the same excuse about healing the boy. They could have said: "*We did everything right, we prayed, we commanded healing, if the boy was not healed, it is God's fault, God didn't want the boy healed!*" But what was Jesus' reaction towards the disciples' inability to heal?

By Jesus' reaction, we see that the disciples had the power and authority to cast the demon out, but they failed to manifest it. Otherwise, Jesus would have never responded to them in such a harsh manner: "*O faithless and perverse generation, how long shall I be with you? How long shall I suffer you?*" Remember Jesus had already given them power and authority over all devils, and to cure diseases as described in **Luke 9:1-6**, **Matthew 10:5-15** and **Mark 6:7-13**. The disciples already had success healing and casting out demons before, and the very fact that afterward they went to Jesus to ask '*why could not we cast the demon out*' shows that this was an unusual event for them. So what happened this time that they could not succeed?

Jesus first answer was: "*Because of your unbelief* *[little faith]"

* from the Greek ³⁶⁴⁰ *oligópistos*: ³⁶⁴¹*olígos*, 'little in number, low in quantity' and ⁴¹⁰²*pístis*, 'faith' - of little faith.

Oligópistos occurs six times in the New Testament, each time with Jesus rebuking the problem of failing to hear His voice as in **Matthew 6:30, 8:26, 14:31, 16:8, 17:20** and **Luke 12:28**. It describes someone dull to hearing the Lord's voice, or disinterested in walking intimately with Him.

Was Jesus saying that the disciples had no faith or such small faith that was not even the size of a mustard seed, because if it was the size of a mustard seed they would have succeeded? Personally I don't believe that Jesus was saying about them lacking faith, because they had faith previously to heal the sick and cast out demons, neither He was saying that the disciples didn't have faith the size of a mustard seed, but that 'somehow' they failed to hear God's voice in that specific event.

The Bible specifically addresses the effects of doubt over faith so let's focus in this important matter.

One mistake I believe Christians often commit is to think of **doubt** as the opposite of **faith**, whereas if when we *have* one, then automatically we *don't have* the other. However, this is not true, according to scriptures. So let's exam it.

Matthew 21:21
Jesus answered and said to them, truly I say to you, **if you have faith, and doubt not,** you shall not only do this which is done to the fig tree, but also if you shall say to this mountain, be you removed, and be you cast into the sea; it shall be done.

If doubt and faith were mutually exclusive, why would Jesus say "*If you have faith, and doubt not*"? If having faith meant automatically not having doubt Jesus would never have said that. Instead, He would have just said "*If you have faith, you shall not only do this which is done to the fig tree…*". The very fact that Jesus mentioned '*if you have faith*' and right after '*and* [if you] *doubt not*' clearly shows a conditional statement; and by His conditional statement we can conclude that even if we have faith, if we also have doubt, we won't be able to do as He did to the fig tree.

Mark 11:23-24
For truly I say to you, that whoever **shall say** to this mountain, be you removed, and be you cast into the sea; and **shall not doubt** [hesitate, waver] **in his heart,** but **shall believe** that those things which he said shall come to pass; he shall have whatever he said. Therefore, I say to you, whatsoever things you desire, when you pray, believe that you receive them, and you **shall have them**.

Here, also in Mark 11, we see the three requirements Jesus taught in order for the mountain to move:

1. Jesus said for us to speak (in faith) **straight to** the mountain.
2. We should not doubt.
3. We should unwaveringly persist in believing, until what we have spoken comes to pass.

A common example of believers having faith and doubt at the same time is when Christians believe (have complete assurance and faith) that God **can** heal, but they are not sure *if* it is God's desire to heal every person in every situation. Because of this, many begin their prayer by saying "*God, if it is your will please heal.*" In this instance, they already began praying with a statement of doubt and unbelief.

James 1:5-8
If any of you lack wisdom, let him ask of God, who gives to all men liberally, and upbraids not; and it shall be given him. But he **must ask in faith, without any doubts**, for the one who has doubts is like a wave of the sea that is driven and tossed by the wind. For let not that man [who doubts] think that he shall receive any thing of the Lord. A double-minded man is unstable in all his ways.

So as the passages of Matthew, Mark and James say, **it is possible for us to have faith and doubt at the same time!**

For us to have the power the Bible says we should have, in my opinion, is not only a matter of *having more* or *bigger faith*, but taking out doubt from our hearts first. When it comes to doubt, there are several different factors involved. Doubt can come from simple ignorance [lack of knowledge of the Truth], but also from a carnal mind which has not been transformed and renewed, but is, instead, grounded in the wisdom of the world. Doubt can also come from the wrong teaching of scriptures that distort the truth of God, and from the lack of revelation of God's nature, love and of His will. As these passages say, **doubt** has the power to cancel

faith, but once doubt has been eradicated, I believe, as Jesus said, just a small amount of faith, the size of a mustard seed, is sufficient to move a mountain.

Many times, Christians will passively ask "*God, increase my faith*" or "*God, give me more faith*," as if it was up to God to decide if He wants or does not want to grant them 'more faith'. Well, even if we really had a problem in lacking faith, we know that faith doesn't come by *asking*, because the Bible says that faith comes by *hearing* [as a continuous act] (**Romans 10:15**) the word of Christ. God won't force His will over our free will if we decide not to be transformed by the renewing our minds (**Romans 12:2**).

Instead of just asking for faith, shouldn't we ask God to help us deal with doubt and unbelief? When we are failing to hear God's voice, as the disciples failed to in **Matthew 17:14-21,** shouldn't we ask God to show us where we are failing? When our experiences don't align with the promises of God in the scriptures, how do we respond? Do we get defensive, proud or doubt God's Word and promises? Do we distort the scriptures to justify our failure? Do we deflect personal accountability? Or, are we humble enough to come before Him and say: "*God I know your Word is true, your promises are true, why didn't I see it manifested?*"

I don't recall seeing in scriptures the apostles, after receiving the Holy Spirit, asking God for *more faith* – an interesting point. Paul prayed for the **Ephesians 1:17-19**:

"*That the God of our Lord Jesus Christ, the Father of glory, may give to you the Spirit of **wisdom** and **revelation in the knowledge of Him**. The eyes of your understanding being enlightened; that you may know what is the hope of His calling, and what are the riches of the glory of **His inheritance in the saints**, and what is the **exceeding greatness of His power to us-ward who believe**, according to the working of His mighty power...*"

Faith is not only a 'gracing' [*gift*] (**1 Corinthians 12**) but is a fruit of the Spirit (**Galatians 5:22-23**). So, whoever is born again [from above], not only has love, joy, peace, long-suffering, gentleness, goodness, meekness, and temperance, but also has faith. The real question is not about whether we have *faith or not*, but **if** we are walking in the Spirit so that these characteristics may be manifested. Power will be manifested in our lives as Christians when we realize our new identity in Christ as new creations, know the authority we have in Him, and start being doers instead of hearers only. As we act and persist in faith, we are going to see the results of it.

'Religion' has divided not only the body of Christ, through denominational sects, but also the teachings of Christ. Faith has been divided into faith for salvation, faith for healing the sick, faith for prophesying, and so on. The 'gracing' [*gifts*] of the Spirit have been divided in such a way that many times it quenches and limits the power of the Holy Spirit to move as He [the Spirit] wills, as if only those with the '*gift*' of prophecy could prophesy, or only those with the 'gift' of healing could heal. We fail to perceive that we already have the **greatest gift of all**, the **Holy Spirit**, who is not only able, but willing (much more than you and I desire) to manifest any of the gifts at any point, to display the works of Jesus through us for the benefit of all.

I don't want to go off topic into **1 Corinthians 12,** or into what we call the 'fivefold ministry', but we need to understand the goal as expressed in **Ephesians 4:11-14**:

"*And he gave some, apostles; and some, prophets; and some, evangelists; and some, pastors and teachers; For the perfecting of the saints, for the work of the ministry, for the edifying of the body of Christ: **Till we all come in the unity of the faith, and of the knowledge of the Son of God, to a perfect man, to the measure of the stature of the fullness*** *of Christ: That we from now on be no more children, tossed to and fro, and carried about with every wind of doctrine, by the sleight of men, and cunning craftiness, whereby they lie in wait to deceive."*

Was Christ just a prophet? Just a healer? Just a teacher or evangelist? No! So, if the same Spirit that raised up Christ from the dead dwells in us, why would we ever say things like, *"I can't heal the sick because I don't have the 'gift' of healing?"* The Bible says we have the mind of Christ (**1 Corinthians 2:16**), we can do all things through Christ which strengthens us (**Philippians 4:13**), and as Jesus himself said in **Matthew 17:20** "[through faith] *...nothing shall be impossible to you."*

Concerning the will and plans of God, Christians often misquote **1 Corinthians 2** by referring only to verse **9** *"But as it is written, eye has not seen, nor ear heard, neither have entered into the heart of man, the things which God has prepared for them that love Him,"* but they forget the most important part from verses **10** to **13** "**But God has revealed them to us by His Spirit**: *for the Spirit searches all things, yes, the deep things of God. For what man knows the things of a man, save the spirit of man which is in him?* **Even so the things of God knows no man, but the Spirit of God. Now we have received, not the spirit of the world, but the Spirit which is of God; that we might know the things that are freely given to us of God. Which things also we speak**, *not in the words which man's wisdom teaches, but* **which the Holy Ghost teaches**; *comparing spiritual things with spiritual."*

Ephesians 1:8-9
Wherein He has abounded toward us in all wisdom and prudence; having made known to us the mystery of His will, according to His good pleasure which He has purposed in Himself.

As we see in these two verses above, the will of God can be known, through the Spirit, as He teaches us all things.

1 John 2:27
But the anointing which you have received of Him stays in you, and you need not that any man teach you: **but as the same anointing teaches you of all things**, and is truth, and is no lie, and even as it has taught you, you shall abide in Him.

John 14:26
But the Comforter, which is the Holy Ghost [*Spirit*], whom the Father will send in My name, **He shall teach you all things**, and bring all things to your remembrance, whatever I have said to you.

Now returning to our main passage, Matthew 17, I would like to make one last observation. As in **Matthew 17:14-21 we** also see in **Matthew 9:27**, **Matthew 15:22**, **Matthew 20:31**, **Matthew 17:15**, people going to Jesus and saying, "...*have mercy* on*..." instead of asking for healing directly.

* from the Greek [1653] *eleeó* which origin comes from [1656] *eleos* meaning: pity, mercy, compassion.

So, we can see the straight correlation between *mercy* and *healing*. If we say our God is merciful, we should believe that He is the same God (Jehovah Rapha) who heals our diseases.

The Will Of God Throughout The Ages

God already showed through Jesus' life and throughout the entire Bible what His will is concerning healing. If you say you don't know God's desire concerning sickness and disease, look to Eden prior to the fall of man.

Genesis 1:26-27 & 31
And God said, let Us make man in Our image, after Our likeness: and let them have dominion over the fish of the sea, and over the fowl of the air, and over the cattle, and over all the earth, and over every creeping thing that creeps on the earth. So, God created man in His own image, in the image of God created He him; male and female created He them.
31 And God saw everything that He had made, and, behold, it was very good.

Adam and Eve lived in a perfect environment – there was no sickness and disease back then. Man was not only a "very good" created being but he was made in God's own image. The root of death was caused by the fall of man; sickness and diseases were a result of sin.

Genesis 2:16-17
And the Lord God commanded the man, saying, of every tree of the garden you may freely eat: But of the tree of the knowledge of good and evil, you shall not eat of it: for in the day that you eat thereof you shall surely die.

Now look to what Revelation says about the new heaven and the new earth. Do you think there will any sickness or disease there?

Revelation 21:4-5
And God shall wipe away all tears from their eyes; and there shall be no more death, neither sorrow, nor crying, neither shall there be any more pain: for the former things are passed away. And He that sat on the throne said, behold, I make all things new...

Just these two examples, from Genesis and Revelation, should be enough to convince you about what God's desire is concerning sickness and disease. Well, you can still ask: "*What about the Earth in which we live in after sin?*"

Since the Old Testament, God had already provided a way for physical healing, through obedience of His Word - His commandments.

Proverbs 4:20-22
My son, give attention to my words; incline your ear to my sayings. Do not let them depart from your sight; keep them in the midst of your heart [*inner man*]. For they are life to those who find them and health [*cure, healing*] to **all** their body.

Psalm 107:19-21
Then they cry to the Lord in their trouble, and He saves them out of their distresses. He sent his word, and healed them, and delivered them from their destructions. Oh, that men would praise the Lord for His goodness, and for His wonderful works to the children of men!

Psalm 103:2-4
Bless the Lord, o my soul, and forget not all His benefits: Who forgives **all** your iniquities; who heals **all** your diseases; who redeems your life from destruction; who crowns you with loving kindness and tender mercies;

Exodus 23:25
And you shall serve the Lord your God, and he shall bless your bread, and your water; and I will take sickness away from the midst of you.

Even in Jesus' time, healing was available for mankind, as we see in the passage of **John 5:2-4**, concerning the pool of Bethesda:

John 5:2-4
Now there is at Jerusalem by the sheep market a pool, which is called in the Hebrew tongue Bethesda, having five porches. In these lay a great multitude of weak folk, of blind, halt, withered, waiting for the moving of the water. For an angel went down at a certain season into the pool, and troubled the water: whoever then first after the troubling of the water stepped in was made whole of whatever disease he had.

Here, God demonstrated His favor and grace towards people, by healing whatever disease from whoever stepped first into the pool after the angel troubled the water. The passage never says that the person needed to be *holy*, *righteous,* or *sinless* in order to receive healing.

How much more right do we have, through faith, to receive healing after Jesus' death? How much more powerful is it to be under the covenant of grace than under the law?

Acts 13:39
Through Him everyone who believes is set free from every sin, a justification you were not able to obtain under the law of Moses.

Romans 10:4
And by Him all that believe are justified from all things, from which you could not be justified by the law of Moses.

Galatians 3:13
Christ has redeemed us from the curse of the law, being made a curse for us: for it is written, cursed is every one that hangs on a tree.

2 Corinthians 5:21
For He has made Him to be sin for us, who knew no sin; that we might be made the righteousness of God in Him.

Praise Jesus for fulfilling the law – being made a curse and sin for us, so we could be justified and made righteous before God!

Christians oftentimes have faith to believe that Christ's death paid for their sins, and that one day they will go to heaven. They don't, however, have the faith to heal the sick, neither do they believe that it is **always** God's desire for people to be healed. Why does that happen? Because, unfortunately, the teaching in churches has been focused almost exclusively on salvation, while ignoring healing. If faith comes by hearing the Word, and you hear only about salvation, that is what you will have faith for.

It may produce believers who will just long for that '*marvelous* day' when Jesus will come back [*the rapture*] to stop all the pain and hurt, but who unfortunately will never experience the power of the Holy Spirit in their daily lives. This is the reason many churches have believers who are just as sick as unbelievers – they lack the knowledge of Christ's finished work on the cross and lack knowledge of the authority they have in Christ.

How important was healing as a part of Jesus' ministry? It is proportional to the importance of physical healing to God.

Sōzō
The Will Of God To Save And Heal

- Does God desire all men to be saved? ☐ Yes ☐ No

- How do you have this assurance? Which scriptures do you use to confirm it?

  If you quoted **1 Timothy 2:3-4** *"This is good, and pleases God our Savior who desires all men to be saved and to come to a knowledge of the truth,"* wouldn't it be wrong for us to pray like this:

  "God show me if it is your will that I preach the gospel to the lost?"

  Or if we are leading a person in a so-called 'sinner's prayer', wouldn't it be wrong for us to pray:

  "God show me if it is your will to save this person?"

  Yes, both prayers above are wrong because we are asking God something He already taught in His word, which is His will. So, we don't have an excuse to pray this way, because it is up to each believer to know God's word.

  So let's analyze **1 Timothy 2:3-4**:

  "This is good, and pleases [*acceptable*] **God our Savior who desires** [*will/wish/want*] **all men to be** *saved* * **and to come to a knowledge of the truth"**.

  * from the Greek [4982] *sōzō* also translated as: **saved, healed, be (made) whole, made well, preserved, rescued.**

[4982] *sōzō* (from *sōs*, "safe, rescued"): deliver out of danger and into safety; used principally of God rescuing believers from the penalty and power of sin – and into His provisions (safety).

Don't you agree that *"rescuing believers from the penalty and power of sin"* means not only salvation, but also includes all sickness and diseases since they are the result of sin?

John 3:17
"For God sent not His Son into the world to condemn the world; but that the world through Him might be **saved** [*sōzō*]."

Let's see three passages where the same word *sōzō* is used as *healed / made whole*:

Matthew 9:20-22 *The woman with the issue of blood*
And, behold, a woman, which was diseased with an issue of blood twelve years, came behind Him, and touched the hem of His garment: For she said within herself, If I may but touch His garment, I shall **be whole** [*sōzō*]. But Jesus turned him about, and when he saw her, he said, Daughter, be of good comfort; your faith has **made you whole** [*sōzō*]. And the woman was **made whole** [*sōzō*] from that hour.

Mark 6:56
And wherever He entered, into villages, or cities, or country, they laid the sick in the streets, and sought Him that they might touch if it were but the border of His garment: and as many as touched Him **were made whole**. [*sōzō*]

Mark 10:51-52
And Jesus answered and said to him, what will you that I should do to you? The blind man said to Him, Lord, that I might receive

my sight. And Jesus said to him, go your way; your faith **has made you whole**. [*sōzō*]

Now Let's meditate on **3 John 1:2**:
"Beloved, I wish [pray] **above all things** that you may prosper and **be in health*, even as**** your soul prospers."

* from the Greek [5198] *hygiaínō*: in good working order - "healthy" in sound condition (in balance). Means to be free from debilitation (incapacity, handicap) functioning holistically with all parts working together (sound). It's opposite of having a debilitating sickness. Thus it became the ideal way to open and close personal letters in ancient times as wishing someone total health.

** from the Greek [2531] *kathōs*: in proportion, to the degree that (J. Thayer); *just as* (in direct proportion), corresponding to fully (exactly).

Isn't it amazing that John attaches the importance of being in (good) health to the prosperity of the soul? And that these two things stand out **above all things**?

So, when we analyze our main verse, **1 Timothy 2:3-4,** through the "lens" of the Greek concordance, we conclude that it can also be read as:

"This is good, and pleases God our Savior who desires all men to be healed" or *"This is good, and pleases God our Savior who desires all men to be made whole"*

If you still doubt that God desires that every person be [physically] healed from sickness and disease, just look to the life of Jesus when He said, *"For I came down from heaven, not to do My own will, but the will of Him that sent me."* Not only that, but if it was not God's desire for every person to be saved and healed, why would Jesus give us the commandment to *preach the gospel to every creature, cast out demons and heal the sick?* Jesus never put any conditions on whom to preach or heal. He never excluded anyone.

It is not God's fault, whether through sovereignty or unwillingness, that people won't receive [*sōzō*] salvation and healing. If people don't want to accept it, believe it or if they are just ignorant of the Truth, they will reap the results of their own free will. It is not up to God anymore to preach the good news and heal the sick...He commanded us to do it. Jesus accomplished everything He needed to on the cross, and then sent us (as apostles) to stand on what He did, under the power and authority given to Him, to perform on Earth the will of God.

Interestingly the Greek term for apostle [652] [*apóstolos*] means: someone sent (commissioned), focusing back on the authority (commissioning) of the sender.

So, in the same way that it's wrong to pray, *"God show me if it is your will that I preach the gospel to the lost,"* it is wrong to pray, **"God show me if it is your will that I pray over the lost to be healed."**

If it is wrong to pray, *"God if it is your will save [sōzō] this person,"* it is also wrong to pray, **"God if it is your will heal [sōzō] this person!"**

Instantaneous Healing [Miracle] And Healing As A Process

Throughout the Bible when we see the accounts of Jesus' healings we can verify that in most of them the healing occurred immediately as He commanded and/or laid hands. The Greek term used in many of the passages is [2112] *eutheós*: immediately, soon, at once.

But for this study we need to mention even the exceptions as we look at four cases mentioned where healing happened in ways that seem more like a process along of a *short* period of time.

Mark 9:25-27
When Jesus saw that a crowd was running to the scene, He rebuked the evil spirit. "You deaf and mute spirit," He said, "I command you, come out of him and never enter him again." The spirit shrieked, convulsed him violently and came out. **The boy looked so much like a corpse that many said, "He's dead."** But Jesus took him by the hand and lifted him to his feet, and he stood up.

Mark 8:23-25
He took the blind man by the hand and led him outside the village. When He had spit on the man's eyes and put His hands on him, Jesus asked, "Do you see anything?" He looked up and said, "I see people; they look like trees walking around." **Once more** Jesus put His hands on the man's eyes. Then his eyes were opened, his sight was restored, and he saw everything clearly. Jesus sent him home, saying, "Don't go into the village."

John 9:6
Having said this, He spit on the ground, made some mud with the saliva, and put it on the man's eyes. "Go," He told him, "wash in the Pool of Siloam" (this word means Sent). **So the man went and washed**, and came home seeing.

Luke 17:14-16
When He saw them [ten leprous men], He said, "Go, show yourselves to the priests." **And as they went, they were cleansed.** One of them, when he saw he was healed, came back, praising God in a loud voice. He threw himself at Jesus' feet and thanked Him — and he was a Samaritan.

So, what conclusions can we get from these four exceptions concerning healing?

- If Jesus needed to lay hands twice for a person to be completely healed, maybe you and I will need to, in some cases, lay hands more than once too. But notice that when Jesus laid hands the first time the person already showed improvement, and so should we.

- Total healing never took a long time to happen, and as the passages indicate, from the time they were in Jesus' presence until the complete healing was manifested, everything may have happened in a matter of hours, at the most.

John 9:6 and **Luke 17:14-16** are two examples where the narrator could have said that Jesus laid hands on the sick people but could not heal them, since they left without the healing manifesting. It's the same way we often mention **2 Timothy 4:20**, where possibly Paul had left Trophimus sick in Miletus.

So let's examine the scriptures!

Paul Left Someone Sick Somewhere...
Didn't He?

2 Timothy 4:20
Erastus stayed in Corinth, and I left Trophimus sick* in Miletus.

* from the Greek ⁷⁷⁰ *astheneó* which can mean *sick* (as disease), but also can mean **weak** as in **Romans 4:19, Romans 14:2, 1 Corinthians 8:12, 2 Corinthians 13:9** and many other verses where the meaning is clearly **weak** not **sick**. The word ⁷⁷⁰ *astheneó* originates from ⁷⁷² *asthenés* meaning: without vigor, strength, weak.

Remember that even Jesus got exhausted physically as in **John 4:6**: "Jacob's well was there, and Jesus, *tired** as he was from the journey, sat down by the well. It was about the sixth hour".

* from the Greek ²⁸⁷² *kopiáō* (from ²⁸⁷³ *kópos*, "exhausting labor"): to labor until worn-out, depleted (exhausted)

Trophimus name is mentioned in two different places in Acts [20:4 and 21:29] accompanying Paul in his third missionary journey dated 54/58 A.D. from Greece, through Macedonia, into Asia, and onward by sea until reaching Jerusalem. After these passages of Acts, we see Trophimus' name mentioned in 2 Timothy 4:20 - the last epistle of Paul dated 66/67 A.D.

- Instead of being sick, could Trophimus have been too exhausted, weak, and without strength to accompany Paul on such long journeys, to the point that Paul needed to leave him in Miletus to rest and recover? ☐ Yes ☐ No

Besides **2 Timothy 4:20**, there is one more passage in the New Testament in which Paul mentions someone close to him who was '770 *astheneó,* and posteriorly received restoration from God, as we read below:

Philippians 2:25-30
Yet I [Paul] supposed it necessary to send to you Epaphroditus, my brother, and companion in labor, and fellow soldier, but your messenger, and he that ministered to my wants. For he longed after you all, and was full of heaviness, because that you had heard that he had been sick [770 *astheneó*]. For indeed he was sick near to death: but God had mercy on him; and not on him only, but on me also, lest I should have sorrow on sorrow. I sent him therefore the more carefully, that, when you see him again, you may rejoice, and that I may be the less sorrowful. Receive him therefore in the Lord with all gladness; and hold such in reputation: Because for the work of Christ he was near to death, not regarding his life, to supply your lack of service toward me.

Yes, here in this passage of **Philippians** we can see the use of the Greek word *770astheneó* meaning more clearly sickness than tiredness. Now meditate on the following questions:

- Can someone's unbelief about the existence of God make God inexistent?

- Can someone's failure to believe God's Word [God's Truth] annul its truthfulness?

- Can someone's failure to manifest the will of God change God's will?

Let's imagine the '*worst case scenario*' as if **2 Timothy 4:20** and **Philippians 2:25-30** really mean that Paul needed to leave Trophimus and Epaphroditus behind in these two different instances due to some kind of sickness or disease that disabled them for a period to continue to minister together with Paul. I am sure that Paul would not have left his beloved friends lacking before praying for them. However, according to **2 Timothy 4:20** and **Philippians 2:25-30** we can infer that they were not immediately healed.

• **Should we conclude that if Paul prayed for them and they were not immediately healed, that it was not God's will for them to be healed?**

Paul was one of the greatest names of the New Testament. He was used mightily by God not only to preach the gospel for the gentiles and perform signs, wonders and even 'unusual' miracles, but also to write nearly 25% of the New Testament. Even with his 'amazing qualifications' could Paul have possibly failed to manifest God's will in healing Trophimus and Epaphroditus?

To be able to respond to this question, one important thing we need to acknowledge when reading the scriptures concerning the life and experiences of the apostles, is that **we need to look to them through the lens of Christ, and His example as the only one who accomplished, perfectly, the will of the Father**. According to what we see in the gospels, what do you think would have happened if Jesus was the one beside Trophimus and Epaphroditus and saw them sick? Would Jesus not have healed them? What if Trophimus and Epaphroditus had gone to Jesus and asked Him to heal them? Would Jesus say, "*Nah man... God doesn't want you healed now, you still need to bear this sickness for a couple of weeks?*"

I don't want to diminish the apostles, nor put them down; they truly were men of God, and we need to respect them for their faithfulness to serve God even unto death. But, we should not forget that Jesus was the only one who never failed to manifest God's will. Before the baptism of the Holy Spirit we see innumerous instances where the disciples failed, like in Matthew 17, where they were not able to heal the demon-possessed boy, Luke 9, where they argued about which of them was the greatest, or Luke 22, where Peter denied Jesus, and John 20, where Thomas doubted Jesus' resurrection, among many other instances.

Someone could say, *"but that was before they had the Holy Spirit living in them, that is why they failed."* Yes, this is correct, the Holy Spirit was **with** them but not **in** them [John 14:17]. But as we look into scriptures we also see the apostles failing to manifest God's will even after the baptism of the Holy Spirit, like in Galatians 2, where Paul rebuked Peter for not walking uprightly according to the truth of the gospel, in Romans 7, where Paul himself was sincere enough to acknowledge that *"for the good that I would I do not, but the evil which I would not, that I do,"* or in Acts 10, where in a vision Peter resisted three times God's command for him to *"kill and eat,"* or in Acts 15, where Paul and Barnabas had a sharp disagreement to the point of separating from each other, and in Acts 16, where Paul circumcised Timotheus, a half-Jew half-Greek, because of the Jews who lived in that area, putting this unnecessary burden on Timotheus even after council concerning the circumcision, as described in Acts 15.

So, before we conclude precipitately that it wasn't God's desire that Trophimus and Epaphroditus be healed, we need to consider the possibility of (even) Paul failing to manifest God's will in his friends' lives as a plausible alternative reason he left them behind.

- **Why do some Christians try so hard to disprove God's truth?**

The Bible warns us about tradition (teachings) created by men:

Mark 7:8
For laying aside the commandment of God, ye hold the tradition of men...

Colossians 2:8
See to it that no one takes you captive through hollow and deceptive philosophy, which depends on human tradition and the basic principles of this world rather than on Christ.

Mark 12:24
And Jesus answering said to them, "do you not therefore err, because you know not the scriptures, neither the power of God?"

Jesus Had 100% Success Healing In His Hometown!

Matthew 13:58
And He   did not many mighty   works there because of   their unbelief.

Mark 6:3-4 (AKJV) & **5-6** (only Strong's)
Is not this the   carpenter, the   son of   Mary,   the   brother of James, and Joses, and of Juda, and Simon?   And are not His sisters here with us? And they were offended* at Him. But Jesus, said unto them, "a   prophet is   not without   honor, but in his own country, and among his own kin, and in his own house."
⁵And He **was not able** there to do not any work of power **if not on a few sick, having laid the hand, He healed** [them]. ⁶And He marveled because of the unbelief of them. And He went out the villages around, teaching.

* from the Greek ⁴⁶²⁴ *skandalizó*: cause to stumble, cause to sin, cause to become indignant, shock, offend.

   This passage, in my opinion, is the one a lot of Christians have a total misconception about - that a person needs to have faith to be healed, as if lack of faith could stop God's healing power.

   Pay attention! The passage does **NOT** say: "*Jesus laid hands on a bunch of the sick people, but only those who believed in him and had faith were healed*".

What I believe it says is: "...because of their unbelief, they didn't come to Jesus for healing; but the few who let Him lay hands were (*all*) healed."

When verse 5 says "*and He was not able...*" it does **NOT** mean "he was not capable" or "he didn't have enough power". Jesus' requirement was not that they needed to have faith to be healed but that they would just come to Him and/or bring the sick! But, because people knew Jesus from childhood and his family, they didn't believe in Him as a prophet (man of God), so they were offended; that prevented them from the possibility of receiving healing through Jesus' laying on of hands.

If faith was required from the person in need of healing for them to receive it, the man at the pool of Bethesda, the beggar at the temple, the centurion's servant, the boy whom the disciples couldn't cast out the evil spirit, would never have been healed, neither would Lazarus and Tabitha had been resurrected. Jesus acknowledged those who came to Him with faith, but also had faith (Himself) and compassion for those who didn't.

I've actually heard from different people who minister healing to others in their daily lives, that it is easier to get a non-believer healed than a believer. This can sound absurd, but maybe it is because a non-believer has nothing to block them from receiving, while a believer can block the healing due to wrong teachings and traditions as in **Mark 7:13**. In cases like this, you should not only pray for the person, but sit down and teach them the truth of the Word of God, and the truth will set the person free and heal them.

So, what is the next common argument that many of 'us' Christians use? Lazarus!

Ok, so let's read and meditate on it!

God's Timing

As I said in the beginning of the book, I don't have the answer for everything, especially when talking about the interrelation between God's (*real*) sovereignty, God's omniscience, and man's free will. This overwhelmingly complex interrelation is something that my limited mind cannot fully comprehend. So, I will focus on the teachings I can grasp from the Word of God.

Yes, God had a perfect time in history to bring forth Jesus into Mary's womb (**Galatians 4:4**), and a perfect time for Jesus to start His ministry around the age of 30 (**Luke 3:23**). Some things in God's plans are unchangeable, while others are conditional and subjected to our free will in how or even whether we answer God's call.

Jeremiah 29:11
For I know the thoughts that I think toward you, said the Lord, thoughts of peace, and not of evil, to give you an expected end.

Psalm 27:14
I had fainted, unless I had believed to see the goodness of the Lord in the land of the living. Wait on the Lord: be of good courage, and he shall strengthen your heart: wait, I say, on the Lord.

Although God has thoughts and plans toward us it doesn't mean they will be fulfilled in our lives. Although God's Word says, '*wait on God,*' it doesn't mean we should be apathetically static, hoping His plan will '*fall from sky*' and be fulfilled.

Lamentations 3:25
The Lord is good to them that **wait for Him**, to the soul that **seeks Him**.

2 Chronicles 7:14
If My people, which are called by My name, shall humble themselves, and pray, and seek My face, and turn from their wicked ways; **then** will I hear from heaven, and will forgive their sin, and will heal their land.

Proverbs 3:5-6 says for us to trust in God with all our heart and lean not to our own understanding, to acknowledge Him in all our ways and (*as a result*) He shall direct our paths. But what will happen if we do not trust in Him, if we lean on our own understanding and do not acknowledge Him in all our ways? What do you think will happen if we do not humble ourselves, do not pray, and do not seek His face? Do you think God's plan will be fulfilled in our lives?

So, when talking about God's timing, concerning healing, it is very easy for a person to justify the lack of results by some cheap 'sovereignty' teaching, by saying, "*well, I did my part; I prayed one time, so if so-and-so was not healed it's because it is not God's timing yet.*" Many of us so boldly blame God for the lack of results, but do we ever stop to think that in His Word, God requires that we seek Him with **all** our heart? Do we doubt God's promises that **everyone** who asks, receives, **everyone** who seeks, finds?

Amos 5:4
For thus said the Lord to the house of Israel, **seek you Me, and you shall live**.

At this point, you may say, "*God will not necessarily heal a sickness or disease, because the most important thing is 'healing the soul' (that is, salvation).*" If you really believe in this statement, then meditate on the following verses:

78

Proverbs 4:20-23
My son, **attend to My words**; incline your ear to My sayings. Let them not depart from your eyes; keep them in the middle of your heart. For they are life to those that find them, and **health*** [*medicine, cure, healing, remedy*] **to all their flesh** [*body*]. Keep your heart with all diligence; for out of it are the issues of life.

* from the Hebrew ⁴⁸³² *marpe* which originates from *rapha*** from where we get the name Jehovah Rapha.

Isaiah 53:4-5
Surely, He took up our infirmities [*sickness*] and carried our sorrows [*pain*], yet we considered Him stricken by God, smitten by Him, and afflicted. But He was pierced for our transgressions, He was crushed for our iniquities; the punishment that brought us peace [*completeness, soundness, health*] was upon Him, and by His wounds we are healed*².

*² from the Hebrew ⁷⁴⁹⁵ *rapha:* heal, cure, physician, make whole.

We have the confirmation for this passage of Isaiah in **Matthew 8:14-17**: "When Jesus came into Peter's house, he saw Peter's mother-in-law lying in bed with a fever. He touched her hand and the fever left her, and she got up and began to wait on Him. When evening came, many who were demon-possessed were ***brought to Him***, and He drove out the spirits with a word and **healed all the sick**. This was to fulfill what was spoken through the prophet Isaiah: "*He took up our infirmities and carried our diseases.*"

God is not holding back any good gift from us; it is up to us to seek Him diligently and receive His good gifts through faith. If you say, "I did everything the *word* of *god* says and it didn't work," what you are really saying is: "The *word* of *god* is not true!" What you should say is, "I did everything **I knew** from the Word of God but I couldn't manifest what it promises." In this way, you are acknowledging the truth about God's Word and His promises, but also your limited knowledge concerning the Word of God - that something you are missing from His Word is what is preventing healing from manifesting. Hopefully, this realization will lead you to desire and seek a deeper revelation of His Word.

So, now let's examine Lazarus; you can read the entire passage in **John 11:1-43**.

Some view this passage in this way: "*... you see ... Jesus stayed two more days where he was, when he could have just spoken a word and healed Lazarus from a distance. Jesus let him suffer longer with the sickness and die on purpose.*" Well, it is not completely wrong to think this way; this is certainly one way to look at the situation, but I won't say it is the best way. Jesus makes the most important point of it all in verse 4, when He says, "**This sickness is not to death**, but [*however, instead*] for [*conferring benefit*] the glory of God, that the Son of God might be glorified thereby". In verse 15 Jesus also said, "And I am glad [*to delight in God's grace*] for your sakes that I was not there, to the intent you may believe [*have faith in*]; nevertheless, let us go to him."

The enemy is the one who comes to steal your health, kill you, and destroy your testimony, not God! Again in this passage, as well as in **John 9:3-4,** we see God taking what the enemy intended for evil and transforming it for good - to His glory.

Many times, in scripture, people misunderstand what Jesus was and is saying - His disciples, *especially* misunderstood His sayings. In looking at the misunderstanding about the '*kingdom of God*' that Jesus was referring to, here in **John 11**, we notice the parallel in Martha's misunderstanding about the resurrection that Jesus spoke about. Martha, as many of us, started with what seemed to be a faith statement, "*Lord, if you had been here, my brother* *would not have died. But I know, that even now, whatever you will ask of God, God will give it you."* When Jesus replied directly, *"Your brother shall rise again,"* Martha misunderstands Jesus, thinking He was talking about the resurrection at the last day - a concept she had preconceived in her mind. Then Jesus explains to her that the power of resurrection was right in front of her, saying, *"I am the resurrection, and the life: he that believes in Me, though he were dead, yet shall he live: And whoever lives and believes in Me shall never die."*

When Jesus commanded to take away the stone, we also see Martha doubting Jesus as she answered, *"But, Lord, by this time there is a bad odor, for he has been there four days."* Her reasoning was carnal in nature, as with many of us when our faith is challenged. Once more Jesus needed to remind her, *"Said I not to you, that, if you would believe [have faith in], you should see the glory of God?"*

Romans 8:6-8

For to be carnally minded is death; but to be spiritually minded is life and peace. Because the carnal mind is enmity against God: for it is not subject to the law of God, neither indeed can be. So, then they that are in the flesh cannot please God.

What can I take from the account of Lazarus' resurrection? I believe God gave us the same authority and power that Jesus had to raise the dead, but if we don't have enough faith to raise the dead as Jesus had, we had better be praying for those in need of healing so they won't die!

Take heed. One can mistakenly use the account of Lazarus to justify one's sickness or disease by believing that being in that state is God's will, somehow. Just know that this line of thinking negates the reality of Christ's finished work on the cross and gives the enemy permission to attack So, be careful! Remember the following verses:

Proverbs 23:7
For as he thinks in his heart, so is he...

Proverbs 18:21
The tongue has the power of life and death, and those who love it will eat its fruit.

Proverbs 13:3
The one who guards his mouth preserves his life; the one who opens wide his lips comes to ruin.

Healing and Grace
Manifesting God's Kingdom

- Why do so many 'good' Christians die of sickness and diseases, having not received healing?

Acts 9:36-37
Now there was at Joppa a certain disciple named Tabitha, which by interpretation is called Dorcas: this woman was full of good works and giving of alms which she did. And it came to pass in those days, that she was sick, and died: whom when they had washed, they laid her in an upper chamber.

Since we have already established that is always God's desire for men to be healed (**1 Timothy 2:4**) and be in health (**3 John 1:2**), we can conclude that people dying of sickness and disease is not God's plan. He does not fail to release healing, but we fail to receive it.

In answering the earlier question, we can look at many factors, such as unbelief, lack of faith, doubt, unforgiveness, sin, etc. But the point I want to emphasize is that 'good' Christians won't receive healing simply based on being 'good.' It isn't dependent on our performance, but **God's grace**.

Oftentimes Christians fall into the trap of works-based faith, believing **they** 'deserve' to receive healing because **they** fast, because **they** pray many hours, because **they** read the Bible every day…focusing on what they **do** instead of focusing on what **Jesus did**, in His righteousness. They may be considered 'good' people who do 'good' deeds but still not know their rights, power, and authority as children of God. We need to be careful to not be confident in our **own righteousness** as described in the parable of the Pharisee in **Luke 18:11-12**: *"God, I thank you, that I am not as other men are, extortionists, unjust, adulterers, or even as this publican. I fast twice in the week, I give tithes of all that I possess."*

What does it take for a person to be saved?

A *novice* Christian would answer this question by just saying "Faith in Jesus Christ," while a more *experienced* Christian would even quote **Romans 10:9-13**:

"That if you shall confess with your mouth the Lord Jesus, and shall believe in your heart that God has raised Him from the dead, you shall be saved. For with the heart man believes to righteousness; and with the mouth confession is made to salvation. For the scripture said, whoever believes on Him shall not be ashamed. For there is no difference between the Jew and the Greek: for the same Lord over all is rich to all that call on Him. For whoever shall call on the name of the Lord shall be saved."

Salvation can be taught just as a simple matter of receiving the grace of God through faith in Jesus Christ. If **grace** is unmerited favor, why do we often attach the grace for receiving healing to our state of being worthy, as if any work we do could give us merit, or as if receiving healing from God depended on our own holiness or sanctification?

I am not saying that we shouldn't read the Bible, or we shouldn't pray or fast, but these things won't make God love us more, nor will they make God give us more 'favor' or 'blessings.' **Reading the Bible, praying, and fasting does not change God's heart toward us, but it changes our hearts toward God, helping us to receive, through faith, what He already gave to us through His grace.**

We were never saved by our own righteousness. Most of us never read the Bible, never prayed, never fasted before accepting Christ into our lives. There was just that beautiful moment when the Holy Spirit convicted us and we realized the grace of God towards *'a sinner like me.'* If salvation didn't demand our 'holy works', why would receiving healing be attached to our performance as Christians?

Now, I am **not** advocating anyone live like the *devil*, sinning boundlessly because of grace (*the Word of God is clear about the consequences of sin*). However, if you live a performance-based Christian life, you will certainly burn out due to living constantly under the condemnation of the enemy, because your performance will never be good enough on its own.

Grace, once understood on a heart level, will never result in an excuse to sin, instead the understanding of grace becomes the empowerment that helps us to desire righteousness, overcome sin, and manifest the new creature we are in Christ.

As we studied, *sōzō (salvation and healing)* is part of the grace of God and as **Titus 2:11** says: *"For the grace of God that brings salvation has appeared to all men."* Although the grace of God for receiving salvation and healing was extended to all men, it does **not** mean that all will automatically receive what is available to them. Otherwise, no one would be condemned. *Sōzō (salvation and healing)* is provided by grace, but received through **faith** as it says in **Ephesians 2:8**: *"For by grace are you saved [and healed] through faith; and that not of yourselves: it is the gift of God."* The appropriation of salvation and healing is not dependent on God but to **our** response through faith towards His grace.

- How do we manifest God's kingdom on Earth?

- What brings the reality of the spiritual realm into the natural realm?

The answer is simply **faith**. Faith is what makes the kingdom of God manifest on Earth as it is in heaven through us. Faith is the bridge that accesses not only grace for salvation, but the power of the Holy Spirit within us, which brings the reality of Jesus' victory on the cross into manifestation in the natural realm in the form of healings, signs, and wonders. Well, in theory every Christian knows the famous verses about faith from **Hebrews 11:1, 2 Corinthians 5:7** and **Romans 10:17**:

"Now faith is the substance of things hoped for, the evidence of things not seen"

"For we walk by faith, not by sight"

"So then faith comes by hearing, and hearing by the word of God [Christ]."

The problem with manifesting faith is not due to the lack of knowledge of theses verses. However, intellectual or 'head' knowledge of scriptures doesn't produce faith. If faith comes by hearing the Word of Christ, and we don't see the works of faith manifested through our lives, we need to consider the truth…that somehow, **we** are failing to hear the true Word of Christ. Surely, we have been sincere in our beliefs, but, unfortunately, we have believed lies, and because of this our faith is not manifesting Christ-like works, as it says in **Romans 3:3-4** and **Hebrews 4:2**:

*"For what if some did not believe? Shall their unbelief make the faith of God without effect? God forbid: **yes, let God be true, but every man a liar**…"*

"For to us was the gospel preached, as well as to them: but the word preached did not profit them, not being mixed with faith in them that heard it."

We need to have faith for healing the same way we have faith for salvation, without overcomplicating the good news. **I believe the missing key for manifesting faith is in the simplicity of the gospel**, as in **2 Corinthians 11:3**: *"But I fear, lest by any means, as the serpent beguiled Eve through his subtlety, so your minds should be corrupted from the simplicity that is in Christ."* That's why Jesus taught us to receive the kingdom of God as little children.

Mark 10:15
Truly I say to you, whoever shall not receive the kingdom of God as a little child, he shall not enter therein.

Matthew 18:3
And said, truly I say to you, except you be converted, and become as little children, you shall not enter into the kingdom of heaven.

- How does a child act when receiving a gift?

A child receives a gift with joy and gladness, never refusing it by thinking *"I don't deserve this gift because I haven't been a good child."* He simply receives his parent's love and gifts. We need to realize that everything God offers us is not because we are lovely, but because **He** is love – not because we are *'holier-than-thou'*, but because His righteousness made us righteous by **His** mercy and grace through faith.

So many Christians have difficulty receiving God's grace and unconditional love, because we grew up in a world which rewards based on performance, and have thus adopted this mindset. Unfortunately, this concept is currently present in the church.

Most Christians will profess and teach things like *'Yes, in order to be saved you just need to believe in Christ,'* and that, *'we are not under the Law anymore, but under grace.'* But, right after a person takes this step of faith and accepts Christ, they create 'new Laws' that say, *"You need to do these things to continue to be accepted in God's sight: You need to read your Bible daily, go to church every Sunday, pay your tithes, pray, fast and serve in a ministry. Unless you do these things, you will not please God, and He won't bless, prosper, heal, or use you through any spiritual gift."*

This mindset is very destructive to the church, because it causes people to look to their own performance, their own works, their own ability to follow X, Y and Z, as a way of justification before God.

Galatians 2:16
Knowing that a man is not justified by the works of the law, but by the faith of Jesus Christ, even we have believed in Jesus Christ, that we might be justified by the faith of Christ, and not by the works of the law: for by the works of the law shall no flesh be justified.

Grace is so unmerited, so undeserving that many will be offended by it, especially the so-called 'religious.' That's why Jesus was so hard on hypocrites, as in **Matthew 23:13**: *"But woe to you, scribes and Pharisees, hypocrites! for you shut up the kingdom of heaven against men: for you neither go in yourselves, neither suffer you them that are entering to go in."*

- Which characteristics of a child do we need to mirror in our Christian life?

1. Dependence: A baby will not survive by himself as he comes out of his mother's womb; he is totally dependent on his parent's care.

John 15:5
*I am the vine, you are the branches: He that stays in Me, and I in him, the same brings forth much fruit: **for without Me you can do nothing**.*

2. Unworried: a child expects there will be food for her next meal, and that her parents are willing to feed her. A normal child is not concerned about the future, about the stock market, about which career to choose, nor about her retirement plan.

Matthew 6:30-31
Why, if God so clothes the grass of the field, which today is, and tomorrow is cast into the oven, shall He not much more clothe you, o you of little faith? Therefore, take no thought, saying, what shall we eat? Or, what shall we drink? Or, wherewithal shall we be clothed? For after all these things do the Gentiles seek: for your heavenly Father knows that you have need of all these things.

3. Joy: A sign of a healthy child is a child who enjoys life, enjoys playing with other children, and having fun. If joy is not present it is a sign that something is wrong with him, and that he needs help.

Romans 15:13
Now the God of hope fill you with all joy and peace in believing, that you may abound in hope, through the power of the Holy Ghost.

4. Trust: A child completely trusts in his parents, having a pure and innocent heart that will believe and learn from their words and example.

Proverbs 3:5-6
Trust in the Lord with all your heart; and lean not to your own understanding. In all your ways acknowledge Him, and He shall direct your paths.

5. Fearless: Once a child acknowledges her parents' love and care, she will trust them enough to not be afraid to do the things they ask, because she knows they would not ask her to do something with the intention of harming her.

1 John 4:18
There is no fear in love; but perfect love casts out fear: because fear has torment. He that fears is not made perfect in love.

6. Belief for the Impossible: Because a child is still not fully trained to have a naturalistic worldview, he will use his imagination to believe the impossible, such as the belief that he has superpowers as the superheroes he watches on TV.

Mark 10:27
And Jesus looking on them said, "with men it is impossible, but not with* God: for with* God all things are possible."

*It is important to highlight that **Mark 10:27** does **not** say 'to' God, it says 'with' God. The Greek preposition translated as with is [3844] *pará* which means from close beside, implying intimate participation.

The first important step for manifesting the kingdom of God is to accept God's grace for what it really is and receive the kingdom of God as a child.

Romans 5:1-2
Therefore *being justified by faith*, we have peace with God through our Lord Jesus Christ: By whom also **we have access by faith into this grace in which we stand**, and rejoice in hope of the glory of God.

Ephesians 2:6
And has raised us up together, and *made us sit together* in heavenly places in Christ Jesus.

   The second step for manifesting God's kingdom is knowing who we are as sons and daughters of God, that is, our identity in Christ and the authority bestowed unto us.

2 Corinthians 5:17
Therefore, if any man be in Christ, he is **a new creature**: old things are passed away; behold, *all things are become new*.

Ezekiel 36:26
A new heart also will I give you, and **a new spirit will I put within you**: and I will take away the stony heart out of your flesh, and I will give you a heart of flesh.

Ephesians 1:3
Blessed be the God and Father of our Lord Jesus Christ, who *has blessed* [*past tense*] us with **all spiritual blessings** in heavenly places in Christ.

   The recognition of our identity in Christ is so key that Satan often tries to deceive us by making us doubt who we are in Christ, to cause us to not manifest the new creature we have become.

   How did Satan challenge Jesus in the desert?

Out of the three ways Satan tempted Jesus, two of them were challenges concerning identity. Satan challenged Jesus not only to doubt who He was but ultimately he tempted Jesus to prove who He was, His identity, by what He was able to perform, that is, by His works, as we see in **Matthew 4** verses **3** and **6**: "*If you be the Son of God, command that these stones be made bread... If you be the Son of God, cast yourself down...*"

Yes, signs follow those who believe (Mark 16:17) and faith without works is dead (James 2:17), but they do **not** define who we are. Rather they are the expression of who God made us to be. If we define ourselves by what we are able to accomplish through our own works, then whenever we are not able to '*perform well*', whenever we pray for someone and the person is not healed, whenever we don't resist the enemy and commit sin, we will tend to doubt or even lose our identity, because Satan will take every opportunity to come with thoughts of accusation, guilt, and discouragement.

God created human '*beings*' not human '*doings*'. Our ability to perform does not define who we are in Christ, but we are defined by our faith in Him. Satan attacks us the same way today and he will have victory if he can cause us to look to ourselves, to our performance, and to our sin and failures, instead of looking to Jesus, His righteousness, His mercy, and His grace.

Healing and Sin
Jesus' Authority

I'd like to just start by saying **Jesus healed sinners.** Sin does **not** stop the healing power of God.

Not one person that Jesus healed in the bible was what we call a *'born again Spirit-filled Christian.'* They didn't need a label to give them a 'special ticket' to receive healing. God is the same yesterday, today and forever, and He wants to heal non-Christians as well as Christians, because He is not a respecter of persons.

Jesus healed all who came to Him, whether the person would follow Him or not, as we see in the account of the ten lepers in **Luke17:11-19**. Healing was not an exchange, a bribe, nor a reward exclusive for those who would decide to follow Him. Healing was, and still is, a manifestation of the goodness of God, and it is up to each person to respond with repentance toward Him once healed. Jesus Himself warned about sin and its effects, even for those who had been healed:

John 5:14
[invalid man in the pool] Later Jesus found him at the temple and said to him, "See, you are well again. **Stop sinning or something worse may happen to you.**"

John 8:11
[adulterous woman] "No one, sir," she said. "Then neither do I condemn you," Jesus declared. "**Go now and leave your life of sin.**"

Matthew 12:43-46

"When an evil spirit comes out of a man, it goes through arid places seeking rest and does not find it. Then it says, 'I will return to the house I left.' When it arrives, it finds the house **unoccupied**, swept clean and put in order. **Then it goes and takes with it seven other spirits more wicked than itself,** and they go in and live there. And **the final condition of that man is worse than the first**. That is how it will be with this wicked generation.

Now let's exam what the Bible says about sin:

Romans 6:23

For the wages of sin is death; but the gift of God is eternal life through Jesus Christ our Lord.

James 1:14-15

But every man is tempted, when he is drawn away of his own lust, and enticed. Then when lust has conceived, it brings forth sin: and sin, when it is finished, brings forth death.

In his letter to the Ephesians, Paul, in chapter 4, warns us about two important things that are attached to each other – not to give place (an opportunity) to the devil and not grieve the Holy Spirit. So, we see Paul warns the **believers (which includes us)** that even though we might be saved and cleansed by Jesus' blood, we still can grieve the Holy Spirit and give a place for the devil to reside and gain victory over us. In **John 14:30** Jesus says that the prince of this world had nothing in Him, i.e., not one foothold, not one accusation against Him.

1 Peter 5:8

Be sober, be vigilant [watch]; because your adversary the devil, as a roaring lion, walks about, seeking whom he may devour.

James 4:7
Submit yourselves therefore to God. Resist the devil, and he will flee from you.

Satan is seeking whom he can devour, because he can't just devour anyone – only those who are not resisting him, and are not submitted to God. Resisting the devil, by itself, without submitting to God results in defeat. The most important aspect of submitting to God is not about obeying *"do's and don'ts,"* as if we were under the law, but submitting the renewal of the mind according to the truth of the Word of God.

Obedience out of obligation or fear will not produce a renewed mind, but a renewed mind will result in obedience out of love.

Matthew 28:18-19
And Jesus came and spoke to them, saying, **all power [*authority*] is given to Me in heaven and in earth.** **Go you** *therefore*, and teach [disciple] all nations, baptizing them in the name of the Father, and of the Son, and of the Holy Ghost:

Right before giving what we call the 'great commission,' Jesus addresses the basis on which His disciples would function, and the foundation of the empowerment in which they would operate. It was because all authority was given to Him in heaven and in earth that '*therefore*' they would be able to do not only the same works of Jesus but even greater.

- If **ALL** power and authority was given to Jesus in heaven and in earth, how much is left to Satan?

Satan had power over mankind not because he was a mighty, fallen angel that had power over creation within himself, but when man was deceived and, subsequently sinned, he empowered Satan by giving him authority to rule over mankind. Therefore, Jesus came…to destroy [*release, unbind, dissolve*] the works of the enemy.

Colossians 2:15
And having spoiled [*completely strip of*] principalities [*rulers*] and powers [*authority, conferred power; delegated empowerment*], He made a show of them openly, triumphing over [*totally defeated*] them in it.

Romans 5:17
For if by one man's offense death reigned by one; much more they which receive abundance of grace and of the gift of righteousness shall reign in life by one, Jesus Christ.

Although Jesus completely defeated Satan, Satan still exerts influence by the only weapon he has left…deception. He has no more authority, but as a thief, he will try to break in where the law is not enforced, and where resistance is not applied. Our ignorance of the scriptures results in a lack of identity as sons and daughters of God, and gives the enemy a foothold to attacks us. Jesus Himself, while being tempted in the desert, resisted the enemy through the Word of God.

It profits nothing for a person to have a million-dollar inheritance in the bank if he doesn't have knowledge of it, because he can't claim his rights and go to the bank to withdraw it. In the same way, Satan works through deception to deprive Christians of knowing who they are in Christ, and of the rights and benefits they have in Him. That is why right teaching of scriptures is vital, as Jesus said in **John 14:15**: "If you love Me, keep [*guard, preserve, keep intact*] My commandments." Jesus and the apostles also warned about false prophets and false teachers, not as people from the outside who appear as wolves, but as people who appear as sheep, even performing signs and wonders (Mark 13:22) but ultimately bring deceptive teachings.

Healing and Faith

Does a person need faith to be healed?

Well, if the person has faith in Jesus to be healed, that is great, but I believe it is **not** a requirement. Yes, Jesus acknowledged all those who came to Him with faith to be healed! Yes, faith pleases God! But how about when the person in need of healing is not a believer, and doesn't have faith in Jesus or is wavering in it? If we believe that faith is required in order for them to receive healing why would we even bother to pray for them?

Many times, Christians put all the burden on the other person, so they can feel justified if nothing happens, as if saying: "*I prayed with all my faith for so-and-so; if he was not healed, it was because of his lack of faith.*" But, how does our own faith play a part and affect the who lacks it? If healing is dependent on the afflicted one's faith, why pray for someone who's in a coma, for example?

Concerning faith, Jesus Himself exalted only two people who came to him with *great* faith – the Centurion (Luke 7:1-10) and the Canaanite woman (John 15:21-28). Ironically, neither of them were Jewish, neither one of them were what we would call '*born again believers*' or people who were rooted in the '*correct religious faith.*'

Mark 16:15-20
He said to them, "**Go into all the world and preach the good news to all creation**. Whoever believes and is baptized will be saved, but whoever does not believe will be condemned. **And**

these signs will accompany those who believe: In My name, they will drive out demons; they will speak in new tongues; they will pick up snakes with their hands; and when they drink deadly poison, it will not hurt them at all; they will place their hands on sick people, and they will get well."

Let's analyze this passage:

- "*Go into all the world and preach the good news to all creation.*" Means: believers go preach to the unbelievers.

- "*And these signs will accompany those who believe...*" Means: signs will follow believers who will place their hands with faith on the sick people to heal them.

- "*...and they will get well*" Means: the unbelievers will get well.

Jesus did not say, "*and they will get well only if they have faith,*" so let's **not** put boundaries where Jesus didn't!

In **Luke 10:8-9** when Jesus sent out the group of seventy to go into every city and place, He didn't create boundaries concerning whom to heal nor did He establish the faith of the afflicted as a prerequisite for receiving healing. Jesus simply commanded His seventy disciples (the ones who were supposed to manifest **their** faith): "*And into **whatever** city you enter, and they receive you, eat such things as are set before you: and* [you] ***heal the sick that are therein**, and say to them, the kingdom of God is come near to you.*"

Jesus challenged the disciples many times about their unbelief, because it is not necessarily up to the person in need of healing to have faith, but for the disciples (those of us who believe) to have it for those in need.

In **Matthew 8:13** and **Matthew 9:29** Jesus made similar statements: "according to your faith be it done unto you" and "as you have believed, so be it done to you," so we need to question ourselves: "*What am I having faith for? What am I believing for?*"

These verses have a twofold implication: first they make **us** responsible for receiving from God according to the way **we** believe, which goes against the belief of some Christians about God's sovereignty, as if He was the one controlling when and how people are healed. If we reverse **Matthew 9:29** we must acknowledge the truth that "as you have *failed* to believe, so it *won't be* done to you." Yes, this makes me uncomfortable, but I personally prefer to be challenged to look where I have been failing in my beliefs, so that I can grow in my faith, as opposed to trying to justify myself at the expense of the truth of His Word.

The second implication of these two passages lies in this statement that, "according to your faith be it done not only **unto you** but also **through you.**" Even though some may say that I am changing the 'original' meaning, I believe it to be true.

James 5:14-15
Is any sick among you? let him call for the elders of the church; and let them pray over him, anointing him with oil in the name of the Lord: And the **prayer of faith** shall save [heal] the sick, and the Lord shall raise him up; and if he has committed sins, they shall be forgiven him.

James 5 does **not** say that the prayer might heal the sick only if it is 'God's will for them to be healed.' It also does **not** say that any prayer will heal the sick, but it guarantees that the prayer when offered in complete faith will heal the sick. This passage never implies the possibility that it may not be God's will to heal. On the contrary, I believe it implies that God desires the person be healed, but with the contingency that someone prays [commands] in faith – a requirement for God's will to be manifested.

At this point you may ask: "*how about the faith of the person who is sick? Don't they also need to believe in order to receive?*" Well, as we just read in **Mark 16:15-2, Luke 10:8-9 and James 5:14-15** there is nothing in these passages that put the onus of faith on the person who is sick; it puts the responsibility on the ones healing the sick. It is also important to note that James 5 does **not** explicitly state that **only** elders could pray for the sick in the church. I believe it points to the idea that we should expect more from them concerning their ability to manifest God's power, since they should be mature in the Word and full of the Spirit. Unfortunately, this is not always the case in all churches.

If it were only up to the person in need to have faith, Lazarus, Tabitha (Dorcas), Jairus' daughter, the widow's son and Eutychus would never have been raised from the dead, because a dead person's faith is of no effect. To reinforce this thought, Jesus talked about faith to the disciples on two different occasions:

Luke 17:6
He replied, "**If you have faith** as small as a mustard seed, you can say to this **mulberry tree**, 'Be uprooted and planted in the sea,' and **it will obey you.**

Matthew 17:20
He replied, "Because you have so little faith. I tell you the truth, **if you have faith** as small as a mustard seed, **you can say to this mountain**, 'Move from here to there' and it will move. Nothing will be impossible for you."

In these two passages, it is very clear that the mulberry tree and the mountain have no faith, at all, but those who are commanding them to move do.

Simply and directly, Jesus said, "*these signs will accompany those who believe.*" So, if signs and healings do not follow us, it is because something is wrong in our belief; otherwise, God would be a liar. God said, "*they **will** place their hands on sick people, and they **will** get well,*" not "*... **maybe** will get well.*"

The following passages show that healing does not depend only on the faith of a person who has a disease, but mainly on the one who intercedes (representing Jesus):

John 5:6-9
When Jesus saw him lying there and learned that he had been in this condition for a long time, He asked him, "Do you want to get well?" "Sir," the invalid replied, "I have no one to help me into the pool when the water is stirred. While I am trying to get in, someone else goes down ahead of me." Then Jesus said to him, "Get up! Pick up your mat and walk." At once the man was cured; he picked up his mat and walked.

The invalid man didn't go to Jesus, didn't ask for healing, and didn't expect Jesus to heal him. Jesus was the one moved with compassion for the man's condition, to go to him and heal him.

Acts 3:1-8
One day Peter and John were going up to the temple at the time of prayer—at three in the afternoon. Now a man crippled from birth was being carried to the temple gate called Beautiful, where he was put every day to beg from those going into the temple courts. When he saw Peter and John about to enter, he **asked them for money.** Peter looked straight at him, as did John. Then Peter said, "Look at us!" So, the man gave them his attention, expecting to get something from them. Then Peter said, "Silver or gold I do not have, but what **I** have [*hold/possess*] **I** give [*offer/minister/grant*] you. In the name of Jesus Christ of Nazareth,

walk." Taking him by the right hand, he helped him up, and instantly the man's feet and ankles became strong. He jumped to his feet and began to walk.

Here in Acts we see the same case – the crippled man never asked for prayer or healing; it was the apostles, who, in their compassion and love, went to him, and set him free from his condition.

What would happen in our churches if someone said, "*I can heal the sick?*" Many would be offended and react by saying, "*You can't heal the sick! God is the one who heals!*"

Interestingly in this passage of Acts the apostle said, "***but what I have I give you.***" Of course, they knew that the power to heal was not **of** themselves, but they understood they had power **in** themselves **at their disposal** to heal, because they were joined to the Lord in one Spirit (**1 Corinthians 6:17**), and partakers of His divine nature (**2 Peter 1:4**), having put on the new man, which God created in righteousness and true holiness (**Ephesians 4:23-24**). That is, they understood that Christ lived in them (**Galatians 2:20**).

It is important to remember how Jesus commanded the disciples (and us) in **Matthew 10:7-8**:

"And as **you** go, preach, saying, the kingdom of heaven is at hand. [*You go*] Heal the sick, [*you go*] cleanse the lepers, [*you go*] raise the dead, [*you go*] cast out devils: freely **you** have received, freely [*you*] give." Jesus **never** said, "You go and **ask Me** to heal the sick, **ask Me to cleanse the lepers, ask Me to raise the dead.**"

So, based on what was presented, should we offer to pray [heal] for unbelievers?

... for those who do not come to church?

... for those who are not asking for help?

... for those who are under Satan's influence and need to be set free?

Waiting For the Leading of the Spirit

If you get the leading of the Spirit to do something specific, do it! But if you don't get it just do the Bible!

Many churches teach that we need a special leading of the Spirit to be able to act on something, as if we would hear an audible voice from heaven or an angel telling us what to do or which person to pray for. I'm not saying that these things can't happen...they can. But many of us use this as an excuse to stay in our comfort zone.

If you are one of those people waiting for the Spirit's 'leading,' I have good news – the Spirit already told you what to do in His Word, the Bible!

"A new command I [*Jesus*] give you: Love one another. As I have loved you, so you must love one another. Go into all the world and preach the good news to all creation, heal the sick, raise the dead, drive out demons. Freely you have received, freely give."

Let's see the example of **Acts 16:6-10**:

"Paul and his companions traveled throughout the region of Phrygia and Galatia, having been kept by the Holy Spirit from preaching the word in the province of Asia. When they came to the border of Mysia, **they tried** to enter Bithynia, **but the Spirit of Jesus would not allow them to**. So, they passed by Mysia and went down to Troas. During the night Paul had a vision of a man of Macedonia standing and begging him, "Come over to Macedonia and help us." After Paul had seen the vision, we got ready at once to leave for Macedonia, concluding that God had called us to preach the gospel to them."

This is the best example showing that God's leading comes **AS** we **DO** the great commission. In Acts 16 we see that Paul didn't stay idle waiting for the "leading of the Spirit" before going out to preach the gospel. Paul was obeying and acting according to Jesus commandments.

Unfortunately, however, many Christians say: "I need to be led by the Spirit," as if unable to do anything until then. Well, if we don't obey what God has already commanded in His Word, nor put faith into practice, we should not expect to receive any leading of the Spirit, either by supernatural vision or dream, nor to be used by God in the spiritual gifts.

Jesus said in **John 6:63** "...The **words** I have spoken to you are **spirit** and they are life." So, if the words Jesus spoke are spirit and we obey His words, we consequently are being led by the Spirit; if we need some "extra" guidance, as Paul did, THEN the Spirit will give us specific leading.

In **Luke 6:46-47,** Jesus says, "Why do you call me, 'Lord, Lord,' and **do not do what I say**? I will show you what he is like who comes to Me and **hears My words and puts them into practice.**

Here's an example: you are in the supermarket and see a person visibly in pain, and suffering. Immediately the battle in your mind begins:

Holy Spirit: "Go pray for that person" *(In a small voice)*
Flesh: "Well, I'm not sure if it is God's will or willing to heal that person!"
Holy Spirit: "Please, go pray for that person"
Flesh: "There are other people around, what they will think of me?"
Holy Spirit: "Trust Me, go pray for that person"

Flesh: "And if nothing happens?"

Holy Spirit: "Obey My command, and go pray for that person"

Flesh: "God, if You want me to go pray give a sign
             from Heaven!"

... After waiting 10 seconds for God's answer...

Flesh: "Well God, You didn't give me the sign from
             Heaven, so You don't want me to pray for
             this person!"

First, I don't think anyone likes to be sick or to have any disease, at all. So, if we at least love others as ourselves, we shouldn't want to see others with sickness and disease either. Right?

- **Christ said for us to love one another as He loved us! How did Christ act toward those who were suffering with sickness, diseases and oppressed by the devil?**

- **Didn't He have compassion, set them free and heal them? So, shouldn't we be doing the same?**

Second, if we can see a person suffering and have compassion on him, think of how much more love and compassion God has for that person to be willing to help him. The simple fact that we can feel any kind of compassion and love, is a sign that the fruit of the Spirit is in us, because love and compassion are not of the flesh.

Galatians 5:16-18 & 22-26
So I say, live by the Spirit, and you will not gratify the desires of the sinful nature. For the sinful nature desires what is contrary to the Spirit, and the Spirit what is contrary to the sinful nature. They

are in conflict with each other, so that you do not do what you want. But if you are led by the Spirit, you are not under law...
... But the fruit of the Spirit is *love, joy, peace, patience, kindness, goodness, faith, gentleness, and self-control*. **Against such things there is no law**. Those who belong to Christ Jesus have crucified the sinful nature with its passions and desires. Since we live by the Spirit, let us keep in step with the Spirit. Let us not become conceited, provoking and envying each other.

With this we can conclude that when we hear "Go pray for that person," we can be sure that it is God's will, and that the Spirit is leading us, because goodness is of God only, and not of ourselves.

If we are acting according to the fruit of the Spirit, we are acting according to God - there is no law against it!

So, the next time we have this battle in our mind, we have no excuses anymore. It is up to **us** to choose which voice to obey!

Signs And Wonders... What For?

A Reason Not To Believe In Jesus

Amazingly, Jesus gave a reason for people to **not** believe in Him. In **John 10:37-38** Jesus said:

"**If I do not the works* of My Father, believe Me not.** But if I do, though you believe not Me, believe the works*: that you may know, and believe, that the Father is in Me, and I in Him."

The works of Jesus bore witness of Him, and healing was an important part of Jesus' ministry, and still an important sign for unbelievers.

John 5:36
But I have greater witness than that of John: for the works* which the Father has given Me to finish, the same works* that I do, bear witness of Me, that the Father has sent Me.

John 14:10-12
Believe you not that I am in the Father, and the Father in Me? The words that I speak to you I speak not of Myself: but the Father that dwells in Me, He does the works*. Believe Me that I am in the Father, and the Father in Me: or else believe Me for the very works* sake. Truly, truly, I say to you, he that believes on Me, the works* that I do shall he do also; and greater [works] than these shall he do; because I go to my Father.

* from the Greek [2041]*érgon*: **a work, deed, action**. A work or worker who accomplishes something. A deed (action) that carries out (completes) an inner desire (intention, purpose).

If our God is supernatural and His Spirit dwells in us, why do many of us live such powerless lives based on the natural?

If no supernatural power is demonstrated through our lives, how can we say that our God is different than the god of the Muslims, of the Hindus, or from witchcraft?

- **How can we say that the Bible is the only true Word of God, if the things it says we're supposed to do don't happen?**

When John the Baptist inquired if Jesus was the One who should come, what did Jesus do?

Luke 7:20-23 (Matthew 11:1-6)
When the men were come to Him, they said, John the Baptist has sent us to You, saying, are You he that should come? Or look we for another? **And in that same hour He cured many of their infirmities and plagues, and of evil spirits; and to many that were blind He gave sight.** Then Jesus answering said to them, go your way, and **tell John what things you have seen and heard; how that the blind see, the lame walk, the lepers are cleansed, the deaf hear, the dead are raised, to the poor the gospel is preached.** And blessed is he, whoever shall not be offended in Me.

The first thing Jesus did was demonstrate the works and the power of God by healing people, then He pointed to the scriptures of **Isaiah 29:18**, **35:4-6** and **61:1** to confirm who He was - His identity.

So, shouldn't we see this as an example of evangelism? Instead of trying to convince unbelievers by the Word only, shouldn't we be accompanied by the demonstration of power, or even as we saw in Luke 7, begin with the demonstration of power first, and then present the Word?

Mark 16:20
Then the disciples **went out** and **preached everywhere**, and the Lord worked with them and **confirmed His word by the signs that accompanied it.**

John 2:23
Now while He was in Jerusalem at the Passover Feast, many people saw the **miraculous signs He was doing and believed in His name.**

John 2:11
This, the first of his **miraculous signs**, Jesus performed at Cana in Galilee. He thus **revealed His glory**, and His **disciples put their faith in Him.**

John 4:45
When He arrived in Galilee, the Galileans welcomed Him. **They had seen all that He had done** in Jerusalem at the Passover Feast, for they also had been there.

John 6:2
And a great crowd of people followed Him because they saw the **miraculous signs He had performed on the sick.**

John 11:45
(after Lazarus' resurrection) Therefore many of the Jews who had come to visit Mary, and had seen what Jesus did, **put their faith in Him.**

Acts 8:6
And the people with one accord gave heed to those things which Philip spoke, hearing and seeing the miracles which he did.

- So, if Jesus ministry was based on preaching the Word AND performing signs, wonders and healings, why do many churches limit their teaching to the preaching of the Word but neglect the power of the Spirit?

2 Timothy 3:5
...having a **form of godliness** but **denying its power. Have nothing to do with them**.

2 Thessalonians 3:6
In the name of the Lord Jesus Christ, we command you, brothers, to **keep away** from every **brother** who is **idle** and does **not live according** to the teaching you received from us.

Luke 11:28
He replied, "Blessed rather are those who **hear** the word of God **and obey it**."

Luke 8:21
He replied, "My mother and brothers are those who **hear** God's word **and put it into practice**."

1 Corinthians 5:4
When you are **assembled in the name of our Lord Jesus** and I am with you in spirit, and the **power of our Lord Jesus is present**...

God already equipped us with his Word and gave us every spiritual gift through the Holy Spirit that we need to represent Christ. It is up to us to seek Him, believe His Word and obey it, putting it into practice.

Ephesians 1:3
Blessed be the God and Father of our Lord Jesus Christ, who **has blessed** us with **all spiritual blessings** in heavenly places in Christ.

An Example To Follow
How To Heal the Sick

What would it look like if when you get a new job, your boss gives you the task of replying to every email in the company's name, but instead you ask the boss if you can reply every time you receive a new email?

Or, what would it look like if a son were to ask his dad to buy him a car, and after the dad buys him the car, he keeps on asking, *"Daddy will you buy me the car?"*

It sounds utterly ridiculous, doesn't it? But, this is what a lot of Christians do when it comes to administering and receiving **healing**.

A great phrase I heard says:
"You should never ask God to do what He told YOU to do, and you should never ask God to do what He has already done"

We all agree that as Christians we should be followers of Jesus, as it says in **1 John 2:6** and **John 13:15**:

"Whoever says he abides in Him ought to walk in the same way in which He walked"

"I have set you an example that you should do as I have done for you"

When Jesus did what He saw the Father doing as He mentions in **John 5:19-20**, He only did what was God's will, otherwise He would have sinned against God.

Let's meditate on the verses below:

Luke 4:40
Now when the sun was setting, all they that had any sick with various diseases brought them unto Him; and He laid His hands on **every** one of them, and healed them.

Matthew 4:23
Jesus went throughout Galilee, teaching in their synagogues, preaching the good news of the kingdom, and healing **every** disease and sickness among the people. News about Him spread all over Syria, and people brought to Him **all** who were ill with various diseases, those suffering severe pain, the demon-possessed, those having seizures, and the paralyzed, and He healed them.

Matthew 8:16-17
When evening came, many who were demon-possessed were brought to Him, and He drove out the spirits with a word and healed **all** the sick. This was to fulfill what was spoken through the prophet Isaiah: "He took up our infirmities and carried our diseases."

Matthew 9:35
Jesus went through all the towns and villages, teaching in their synagogues, preaching the good news of the kingdom and healing **every** disease and sickness.

Acts 10:38
How God anointed Jesus of Nazareth with the Holy Spirit and power, and how He went around doing good and healing **all** who were under the power of the devil, because God was with Him.

Matthew 10:15
He called his twelve disciples to Him and gave them authority to drive out evil spirits and to heal **every** disease and sickness.

By observing and learning about Jesus' life I would like to ask:

- Where in the Bible do we ever see Jesus **praying** for the sick?

Jesus never '*prayed*' for the sick, He simply healed them. In the same way, He never commanded His disciples to *pray* for the sick but to *heal* the sick. Many Christians see a 'prayer' for healing as a petition to God – as trying to convince Him to *release healing from heaven*. Jesus never prayed to God, so God would heal the sick; Jesus Himself healed. Neither did He ask God if it was God's desire to heal someone before actually healing them, because Jesus already knew God's heart concerning healing. So, if Jesus never did these things, why do so many Christians say [*pray*] things like:

"Father God **if** it is your will heal *so-and-so*..."
"God, in the name of Jesus I **ask You** to heal *so-and-so*..."

Jesus never said for us to ask God to move the mountain or the mulberry tree, but for **us** to speak directly to it - **to command** the mountain and the mulberry tree to move.

Before you say that Jesus prayed to God to resurrect Lazarus, read carefully that passage **John 11:41-42**: "*Father, I thank you that you have heard Me. I knew that You hear Me always: but because of the people which stand by I said it, that they may believe that you have sent Me.*" Jesus didn't pray to God asking God to resurrect Lazarus, but He prayed in a manner that would cause the people to believe. Here, as in all other healing accounts, He just commanded "*Lazarus, come forth.*"

"*But*" Is Not From God, It Is Evil

2 Corinthians 1:20
"For *all the promises of God* in Him are **yes**, and in Him **amen**, to the glory of God by us."

Matthew 5:37
But let your communication (logos) [*word / statement / speech*] be, **yes**, **yes**; **no**, **no**: for whatever is more than these comes of evil.

If God says for our word to be '*yes, yes*' '*no, no*', why would we ever say that His Words and promises are '*maybe?*'

The average Christian would answer the question "*Does God desire to heal sickness and disease?*" by saying things like,

"*...well... sometimes God heals, but sometimes...*"

It is absurd for Christians to think that God would require from them a higher standard than He, Himself, is not able to fulfill. God's promises are "*Yes and Amen*" and not "*Yes, but...*".

This might shock many people, but Jesus Christ is **not** healing a single person on Earth from heaven. He is **not** going back to the cross every time a person needs salvation or healing. Christ's work on the cross has accomplished everything we would ever need, which is why He said, "**It is finished**" instead of "**to be continued**." Our part is not to beg God, as if we were trying to persuade Him to heal someone, but to believe in what has already been done and act by faith in what He commanded us to do having appropriated what was given to us at Christ's expense.

Power of Words

Although there are no formulas for healing, we need to learn from Jesus the principles He used to heal: Jesus used words, commanding sickness and disease to leave. He never talked *to God about the problem,* but talked *straight to the problem* and commanded what He wanted to be done. Let's meditate on the following verses concerning the power of words:

Hebrews 11:3
Through faith we understand that the worlds were framed by the word of God, so that things which are seen were not made of things which do appear.

Psalm 33:9
For He spoke, and it was done; He commanded, and it stood fast.

Proverbs 18:21
Death and life are in the power of the tongue: and they that love it shall eat the fruit thereof.

Matthew 12:37
For by your words you shall be justified, and by your words you shall be condemned.

Laying On Of Hands

Another important principle used to heal the sick was the laying on of hands. The Old Testament mentality was that if someone unclean touched a *'clean'* person they also would become unclean. The New Testament inverts this paradigm: whoever is unclean and touches someone who is clean becomes clean, as demonstrated by Jesus and the apostles. Considering this, allow me to correct a widely misguided teaching about the laying on of hands:

1 Timothy 5:22
Lay hands suddenly on no man, neither be partaker of other men's sins: keep yourself pure.

Many Christians (wrongly) believe that **1Timothy 5:22** is a 'warning' concerning laying hands on the sick, or on the demon possessed as if the sickness or the 'spirit' which is in the other person could somehow be transferred to the Christian. That's total nonsense! If "greater is He that is in us, than he that is in the world" (**1 John 4:4**) is true, why would we ever be afraid of such a thing? In context, the laying on of hands in **1Timothy 5:22** means ordaining people into positions of leadership in the church, as also stated in **1Timothy 3:10**: *"And let these also first be proved; then let them use the office of a deacon, being found blameless."*

Once we have corrected this misunderstanding that creates so much fear in the believer, we can continue to read the passages concerning the laying on of hands.

Luke 4:40
Now when the sun was setting, all they that had any sick with diverse diseases brought them to Him; and He **laid His hands on every one of them, and healed them.**

Luke 13:12-13
And when Jesus saw her, He called her to Him, and said to her, woman, you are loosed from your infirmity. And He laid His hands on her: and immediately she was made straight, and glorified God.

Mark 6:5
And He could there do no mighty work, save that He laid His hands on a few sick folk, and healed them.

Acts 28:8
And it came to pass, that the father of Publius lay sick of a fever and of a bloody flux: to whom Paul entered in, and prayed, and laid his hands on him, and healed him.

Mark 16:18
They shall lay hands on the sick, and they shall recover.

Anointing With Oil

Although there are no records in the Bible of Jesus Himself anointing any person with oil, there are two passages in the New Testament that address this issue.

Mark 6:12-13
And they went out, and preached that men should repent. And they cast out many devils, and anointed with oil* many that were sick, and healed them.

James 5:14-15
Is anyone among you sick? Let them call the elders of the church to pray over them and anoint them with oil* in the name of the Lord. And the prayer offered in faith will make the sick person well; the Lord will raise them up. If they have sinned, they will be forgiven.

* from the Greek [1637] *élaion:* olive oil; (*figuratively*) the indwelling (*empowering*) of the Holy Spirit.

Hebrews 1:8-9 (Psalms 45:7)
But to the Son he said, Your throne, o God, is for ever and ever: a scepter of righteousness is the scepter of Your kingdom. You have loved righteousness, and hated iniquity; therefore God, even Your

God, has anointed You with the oil of gladness [*exuberant joy*] above Your fellows.

In the New Testament, we see the act of anointing with oil as a common practice used for different purposes. Oil was used as a healing agent as described in **Luke 10:34**: "*And went to him, and bound up his wounds, pouring in oil and wine, and set him on his own beast, and brought him to an inn, and took care of him.*"

Anointing the head with oil was also a sign of courtesy towards an honored guest, meant to refresh and comfort after their journey under the sun. An example is in **Luke 7:46**: "*My head with oil you did not anoint: but this woman has anointed My feet with ointment.*"

In biblical times, the oil was used as a symbolic reminder of God's healing power, and a reminder of the spiritual reality, an encouragement to faith. The oil itself has no power to heal; only faith released through or towards the Holy Spirit heals. Can oil be used nowadays? Yes, if you think it will somehow contribute to building up faith. If the Holy Spirit instructs you to use it in a specific situation, by all means, obey and use it. Is it a requirement? No. If we stop praying (*healing*) for the sick because we don't have oil to anoint them, we have made an idol out of it, and have ignored or diminished the power of the Holy Spirit within us. We can view anointing oil in the same way we view the cross as a symbol. It is a reminder of the sacrifice of Christ for us. However, the moment we put our faith into the object, the 'cross,' it becomes an idol.

Acts 10:38

How God anointed Jesus of Nazareth with the Holy Ghost and with power: who went about doing good, and healing all that were oppressed of the devil; for God was with Him.

Don't Limit God

Let's be careful to not limit God. We should be listening to the Holy Spirit, and flowing with the ways in which He wants to move in each situation. For example, Jesus Himself used different ways to heal people with blindness. In **John 9** Jesus spit on the ground, made some mud, put it on the man's eyes and told him to go wash in the Pool of Siloam. In **Mark 8** Jesus took the blind man by the hand and led him out of the town, then He spit straight on the man's eyes, laid hands on him and asked him what he saw. Noticing that the man's sight was not completely restored, He laid His hands on the man's eyes one more time, then his sight was restored. In **Matthew 20** Jesus touched the eyes of two blind men and they immediately received sight.

Humankind loves to create formulas and patterns that can be repeated to get the desired results, because it's easy and comfortable. We ought to be careful that these patterns don't become limits and hindrances for the Holy Spirit to move, in the same way that routine traditions make the Word of God of no effect. Many Christians even turn the *'Lord's prayer'* into an idol, as if the mere repetition of the words would make it effective.

Healing the sick is not a matter of saying *'the right words'*, or *'the right prayer.'* It is not a matter of **what** to say, but **who** says it, the flesh, or the Spirit – manifesting unbelief or faith. I would even go further and say that healing the sick is not even a matter of commanding [*saying/praying*] or laying hands, but believing. Sometimes we can focus too much on 'technique' when it comes to healing. Consider the examples of the apostles Peter and Paul:

Acts 5:14-16
And believers were the more added to the Lord, multitudes both of men and women. So that they brought forth the sick into the streets, and laid them on beds and couches, that at the least the

shadow of Peter passing by might overshadow some of them. There came also a multitude out of the cities round about to Jerusalem, bringing sick folks, and them which were vexed with unclean spirits: and they were healed every one.

Acts 19:11-12
And God worked special miracles by the hands of Paul: So that from his body were brought to the sick handkerchiefs or aprons, and the diseases departed from them, and the evil spirits went out of them.

So, if there are no formulas, what should we do? Which method should we use? I would say use the one you have faith in or the method the Holy Spirit instructs you to use.

Mark 9:23
... all things are possible to him that believes [*to the one believing*].

John 11:40
... Said I not to you, that, if you would believe, you should see the glory of God?

Final Thoughts

Many ideas, concepts, and thoughts were presented in this book, and I realize that some people may not agree with all of them. My purpose in all of this is to share with you the way I understand the scriptures so far in my personal walk with God. As I expressed in the beginning of the book, it is up to each of us to seek the Holy Spirit, and the Word of God, in our search for truth and revelation, since each of us are accountable to God. I hope and pray God's best over your life, that you may never stop growing in Him, in the knowledge of His Word and in intimacy with His Spirit, so that you can manifest His love and grace.

Luke 2:40
And the child grew, and waxed [*became*] strong in spirit, (*being*) filled with wisdom: and the grace of God was on Him.

Luke 2:52
And Jesus increased [*advanced*] in wisdom and stature, and **in favor** [*grace*] with God and man.

As the Bible says, *even* Jesus went through a process in which he became strong in the Spirit and increased in favor with God. So, we also go through this process, as Paul the apostle states in **2 Corinthians 3:18**: "But we all, with open face beholding as in a glass [*mirror*] the glory of the Lord, are changed [*are being transformed*] into the same image from glory to glory, even as by the Spirit of the LORD."

As we advance in our walk with God, I would like to finish by encouraging you with the following verses:

Galatians 6:9
And let us not be weary in well doing: for in due season we shall reap, if we faint not.

2 Corinthians 9:6
But this I say, he which sows sparingly shall reap also sparingly; and he which sows bountifully shall reap also bountifully.

Hebrews 11:6
But without faith it is impossible to please Him: for he that comes to God must believe that He is, and that He is a rewarder of them that diligently seek Him.

www.ingramcontent.com/pod-product-compliance
Lightning Source LLC
LaVergne TN
LVHW051418080426
835508LV00022B/3142